THE
MYTH
OF A CHRISTIAN
RELIGION

Also by Gregory A. Boyd

The Myth of a Christian Nation

GREGORY A. BOYD

Author of *The Myth of a Christian Nation*

THE
MYTH
OF A CHRISTIAN
RELIGION

LOSING YOUR RELIGION
FOR THE **BEAUTY** OF A **REVOLUTION**

ZONDERVAN®

ZONDERVAN.com/
AUTHORTRACKER
follow your favorite authors

The Myth of a Christian Religion
Copyright © 2009 by Gregory A. Boyd

This title is also available as a Zondervan ebook. Visit www.zondervan.com/ebooks.

This title is also available in a Zondervan audio edition. Visit www.zondervan.fm.

Requests for information should be addressed to:

Zondervan, *Grand Rapids, Michigan 49530*

Library of Congress Cataloging-in-Publication Data

Boyd, Gregory A., 1957 –
    The myth of a Christian religion : losing your religion for the beauty of a revolution /
Gregory A. Boyd.
      p.   cm.
    Includes bibliographical references (p. 218).
    ISBN 978-0-310-28383-6 (hardcover, jacketed)
     1. Christian life. 2. Jesus Christ — Example. I. Title.
BV4501.3.B695   2009
243 — dc22   2009001951

Interior design by Beth Shagene

Printed in the United States of America

09 10 11 12 13 14 15 • 23 22 21 20 19 18 17 16 15 14 13 12 11 10 9 8 7 6 5 4 3 2 1

This book is dedicated to Michael and Jean Antonello;
two spiritual pilgrims who know firsthand
that to join the beautiful revolution,
you've got to
lose your religion.

Thank you for your steadfast love
and unwavering encouragement
over the years.

CONTENTS

INTRODUCTION

O<small>NCE UPON A TIME</small> I <small>EMBRACED THE</small> C<small>HRISTIAN RELIGION.</small>

Frankly, I wasn't very good at it. Religion just isn't my thing. For a while I felt like a failure. Some religious folk consigned me (and *still* consign me) to the fire. But over time I've come to see my religious failure as a tremendous blessing.

Because when I lost my religion, I discovered a beautiful revolution.

This may surprise or even offend you, but Jesus is not the founder of the Christian religion. True, a religion arose centuries after he lived that was called "Christian," but as you'll discover in this book, in many respects this religion was antithetical to what Jesus was about. In fact, as you'll also discover in this book, the very concept of a "Christian religion" is something of a myth when understood in the light of what Jesus was about.

What Jesus was about had nothing to do with being religious. Read the Gospels! He partied with the worst of sinners and outraged the religious. This is what got him crucified.

What Jesus was about was starting a revolution. He called this revolution "the Kingdom of God."

This revolution isn't centered on getting people to believe particular religious beliefs and engage in particular religious behaviors, though these may be important, true, and helpful. Nor is it centered on trying to fix the world by advocating the "right" political causes or advancing the "right" national agendas, though these may be noble, righteous, and effective.

No, the Kingdom of God that Jesus established is centered on one thing, and one thing only: manifesting the beauty of God's character and thus revolting against everything that is inconsistent with this beauty. The Kingdom is centered on displaying a beauty that revolts.

The Kingdom, in short, is a beautiful revolution.

Everything about Jesus manifested this beautiful and "revolting" Kingdom. We see it most profoundly when Jesus allowed himself to be crucified. On Calvary Jesus puts on display the beauty of God's decision to suffer for his enemies—and at the hands of his enemies—rather than use his omnipotent power to violently defeat them. On Calvary we also see God's revolt against our enslavement to violence and everything else that keeps us estranged from God and one another. The devil himself is confronted and overcome by the cross of Jesus Christ.

Jesus' death sums up the theme of his whole life. Every aspect of his life, teachings, and ministry put the beauty of God's reign on display and revolted against some aspect of the culture that contradicted this reign.

The central call of all who pledge their life to Christ is to join this beautiful revolution and to therefore humbly live and love *like this*. "Whoever claims to live in him," John says, "must live as Jesus did" (1 John 2:6). We're to manifest God's beauty by sacrificially loving our enemies, serving the poor, feeding the hungry, freeing the oppressed, welcoming the outcast, embracing the worst of sinners, and healing the sick, just as Jesus did. And there's no way to do this without at the same time revolting against everything in our own lives that keeps us self-centered, greedy, and apathetic toward the plight of others. Nor is there any way to do this without revolting against everything in society—and, we shall see, in the spiritual realm—that keeps people physically, socially, and spiritually oppressed.

So you see, the Kingdom has nothing to do with religion—"Christian" or otherwise. It's rather about following the example of Jesus, manifesting the beauty of God's reign while revolting against all that is ugly.

It's a beautiful revolution that we're all invited to join. But to do so, we're got to lose our religion.

CHAPTER 1

GIANT JESUS

Whoever claims to live in him
must live as Jesus did.
1 JOHN 2:6

CONFESSIONS OF A SKEPTICAL PASTOR

Traditionally, Christians have believed that the Church is God's main vehicle for carrying out his will "on earth as it is in heaven." In my early years as a Christian, I was convinced this was true. But over the years I've lost confidence in this—which is a little strange, I suppose, since I'm the pastor of a fairly large evangelical church.

The seeds of doubt were planted in my college years when I first studied the Church's bloody history. Almost all varieties of the Church—Catholic, Lutheran, Reformed, Orthodox, and so on—tortured and murdered people "in Jesus' name." How could this be if the Church is God's main "vehicle of salvation"?

During that time I also became aware of how central following the example of Jesus is to the New Testament's understanding of what it means to "be saved."[1] This slowly opened my eyes to the radical contradiction between the lifestyle Jesus calls his followers to embrace, on the one hand, and the typical American lifestyle, on the other. Yet it struck me that the Church in America largely shares—even celebrates—the typical American lifestyle. Research confirms that the values of Americans who profess faith in Christ are largely indistinguishable from the values of those Americans who do not. How could this be if the Church is God's main "vehicle of salvation"?

Finally, what caused my confidence in the Church to bottom out completely was a movement that arose in the 1980s known as "the Moral Majority." Christians in this movement tried to grab political power in order to "bring America back to God," as they put it.

I've never understood what godly period of American history these folks were trying to get us back to. Was it before or after white Europeans enslaved millions of Africans and slaughtered millions of American Indians to steal their land?

But what really horrified me was *how* they were trying to take America back there (wherever "there" might be). The leaders of this movement called on all "moral" people to side with them in their political crusade against all those they considered "immoral"— liberals, homosexuals, feminists, abortionists, secularists, and the like. Worst of all, many of these leaders did this explicitly "in Jesus' name," while many, if not most, conservative churches jumped on the bandwagon.

What I never understood was why followers of Jesus would try to gain political power over people when Jesus himself never attempted such a thing. Nor could I understand how these Christians could act as if their sins were less serious than the sins of those they were crusading against. Jesus and Paul explicitly taught disciples to embrace the opposite attitude. Followers of Jesus are to consider themselves "the worst of sinners" (1 Timothy 1:15–16) and to maximize their own sins while minimizing the sins of others (Matthew 7:1–3).

This movement also struck me as dangerous. If history teaches us anything, it's that religion and politics make perilous bedfellows. The worst evils in history have occurred when religious people —including Christians—acquired political power. The Crusades, Inquisition, witch hunts, and inter-Christian wars throughout Church history, in which millions were slaughtered "in Jesus name," were all built on this poisonous alliance.

This same history teaches that mixing politics and religion is disastrous not only for nations but for advancing the Christian faith as well. Go to any country where Christians once ruled and you'll find the Church has all but disappeared and the people are generally more resistant to spiritual discussions than those in other cultures.

History teaches that the best way to destroy the Church is to give it political power.

Worst of all, people in the Moral Majority seemed to imply that agreeing with a particular political position was a precondition to entering into the Kingdom of God. Indeed, it justified all who rejected the Moral Majority's political posturing to also reject Christ. It transformed a beautiful Gospel into something that could be easily dismissed and understandably disdained.

If I'd been offered this version of Christianity as a nonbelieving teenager, I'm quite certain I would have remained a pagan.

While the Moral Majority eventually died out, its mindset did not. The first two elections of the third millennium brought forth as much divisive religious posturing as anything that happened in the 1980s or '90s.

Like most evangelical pastors of megachurches, I received an unprecedented amount of pressure to "steer the flock" toward reelecting George Bush in 2004. Most of this came from members of my own five-thousand-person congregation who were getting worked up into a political frenzy by Christian leaders on television, on the radio, on the Internet, and in the mail.

I decided to use the occasion as a teaching opportunity. I would explain the biblical reasons why our church never has, and never will, participate in political activity (as well as why we don't have a flag on our premises, sing patriotic hymns, celebrate the Fourth of July, or do other things like that). So I delivered a four-part sermon series titled "The Cross and the Sword" that spelled out the difference between the Kingdom of God, which followers of Jesus are called to promote, and the kingdoms of the world, which politics concerns itself with.

The messages exposed a division in my congregation that ran through the entire evangelical community. On the one hand, I'd never received such positive responses to anything I'd ever preached.

Some people literally wept for joy, feeling that the Gospel had been hijacked by American politics. On the other hand, roughly a thousand people walked out.[2]

Looking back, I know I could have been more tactful (never my strong suit). But the mass exodus also revealed the ongoing fusion of faith and politics in American evangelicalism—and mine was a congregation that had always taken care to keep the two separate!

THE DISCOVERY OF THE KINGDOM

I might have fallen into incurable cynicism, and even left the ministry, had it not been for one thing: God had been teaching me that the Kingdom of God not only can't be identified with any political party, ideology, or nation; it also can't be identified with any human institution, including the Church, or any organized religion, including Christianity. Rather, the Kingdom of God displays the beautiful character and behavior of the One who first embodied it. It always looks like Jesus—loving, serving, and sacrificing himself for all people, including his enemies.

To the extent that any individual, church, or movement looks like that, it manifests the Kingdom of God. To the extent that it doesn't look like that, it doesn't.

It's that simple.

This insight saved my spiritual life and reignited my passion to be a follower of Jesus.

My hope and prayer is that it will do the same for all who read this book.

THE KINGDOM

Everywhere Jesus went he proclaimed "the Kingdom of God." It's the thread that connects all his teaching. A *kingdom* is any area where a particular king reigns. Literally, it's the *king's domain*. So the Kingdom of God that Jesus referred to is the domain of God's reign. Jesus' life and teachings focused on revealing what it looks like when God reigns in a person's life and in the life of a community.

Jesus didn't just *focus* on the Kingdom, however. He *was* the Kingdom. According to the New Testament, Jesus was the embodiment of God—he was *God Incarnate*, to use traditional terminology. He was, therefore, the very embodiment of the Kingdom of God.

This is one reason why Jesus announced that the Kingdom was at hand wherever he went. It was at hand, because he was there.

As the embodiment of the Kingdom, Jesus didn't just reveal what it looks like. He brought it to us. Through his life, ministry, death, and resurrection, Jesus established the Kingdom in this world. Each time a person submits to God's reign, the Kingdom grows a little more. God's ultimate goal, which he promises to accomplish eventually, is for the whole earth to become a domain over which he lovingly rules.

Our job, as people who submit to God's reign, is to do everything we can to grow this mustard seed Kingdom in our own lives and throughout the world. We're to pray and live in such a way that we bring about God's will "on earth as it is in heaven."

Jesus came to plant this Kingdom. Through his Spirit working in the lives of all who submit themselves to him, he's expanding it. This is what Jesus was and is all about. And this is what we who have pledged our lives to Christ are to be all about. We're to be the Kingdom and to be used to expand the Kingdom.

BELIEFS AND PLEDGES

It's never hard to tell where the Kingdom is advancing and where it's not. Where it's taking hold of people's lives, they increasingly live like Jesus. Where the Kingdom is not present, they don't.

This contrasts sharply with what a lot of people today think Christianity is all about. Many Christians, for instance, seem to think Christianity is mainly about *believing* certain things. If you believe Jesus died for your sins, you're "saved." If you don't, you're "damned." Since we're saved by "faith alone" and not "works," how one actually lives isn't centrally important in this model of Christianity.

Perhaps this explains why so many Americans who profess faith in Jesus have lifestyles that are indistinguishable from their nonbelieving neighbors.

Now, I certainly agree Jesus died for our sins and that we're saved by faith, not works, but the idea that Christianity is primarily about *believing* certain things is seriously misguided. Since Scripture calls Christians "the bride of Christ," try thinking about it this way: to be married to my wife, I certainly need to believe certain things. I need to believe my wife exists, for example. I also need to believe she'll keep her vows to me. But merely believing these things doesn't make me married to her. Believing those things are preconditions for my relationship with her, but they are not themselves the marriage relationship.

I'm married to my wife only because I'm willing to act on my beliefs by pledging my life to her and living faithful to this pledge every day of my life. This doesn't mean my marriage is based on "works," as though I had to earn my wife's love every day. Rather, living faithful to my vows is simply *what it means* to be married.

In the same way, we need to believe certain things to be Christian. We must accept that Jesus exists, for example, and that God will faithfully keep his word. But merely believing these things doesn't make us "the bride of Christ." These beliefs are the precondition for a marriage-like relationship with God, but they are not themselves the relationship.

We become the "bride of Christ" only when we act on our beliefs by pledging our lives to him and living faithful to that pledge every day. This doesn't mean we're saved by "works," as though we had to earn God's love. Rather, living faithful to one's pledge to God is simply *what it means* to be married to him. It's *what it means* to submit to God's reign. It's *what it means* to belong to God's Kingdom.

And as we do this, we increasingly look like Jesus.

Over the last several years the media has coined the term *red-letter Christians* to refer to believers who believe they're supposed to obey Jesus' teaching and live as he lived. (Some Bibles print Jesus' words in red—hence the term *red letter*). What we've seen so far is that there is, in reality, no other kind of Christian. Obeying what Jesus taught and living as he lived is simply what the term "Christian" means.[3]

EXPERIENCING KINGDOM LIFE

Living under the reign of God, as modeled by Jesus, is as contrary to the ordinary way of doing life as anything could be. It's far more radical and countercultural than most people realize, so much so that it would be impossible for someone to live this way by their own power. This brings us to the center of what the Kingdom is all about.

I've said that the Kingdom is not primarily about beliefs, for by definition it redefines how we live. But this doesn't mean the Kingdom is primarily *about* how we live. Rather, the reign of God redefines how we live because it does something even more fundamental within us: it gives us a whole new *kind of Life*. (Throughout this book I'm going to capitalize *Life* when referring to this new kind of Life in order to distinguish it from mere biological or social life.)

When we submit to the reign of God by pledging our life to him, he gives us eternal Life. This Life participates in the beautiful Life of God. It is the abundant Life Jesus said he came to give us. It's the only kind of Life that satisfies our innermost need to experience profound love, worth, significance, and security. It's the Life we were created to share with God.

The Kingdom is about living in a radically new way only because it's first and foremost about participating in a radically new kind of Life. Followers of Jesus live and love like Jesus only because they participate in the fullness of Life Jesus unleashed into the world. Every Christlike thing Kingdom people do simply manifests the Life of Jesus that Kingdom people participate in.

GIANT JESUS

New Testament writers express the truth that the Kingdom is about participating in the Life of God by referring to Jesus followers as "the body of Christ."

Jesus acquired an ordinary body when he was born in Bethlehem, but now he has acquired a collective body with the Church.[4] The Church is his hands, mouth, and feet operating in the world today. The same Life that was in his first body is in us, his second body. And we who belong to this second body take our marching orders from the same "head" as Jesus' first body.

This is why Luke begins his work on the history of the early church by reminding his readers that in his earlier written Gospel he "wrote about all that Jesus began to do and to teach until the day he was taken up to heaven" (Acts 1:1). To say that Jesus "began" to do certain things in his incarnate form implies that Jesus is now continuing to do certain things in a corporate form—through his Church. In Luke's mind, his Gospel was about what Jesus did through his first body, while the book of Acts is about what Jesus continued to do through his second, corporate body.

In other words, Luke sees the Church as a sort of giant Jesus. And this giant Jesus is still ministering to the world today.

In the book of Acts you can also see that Jesus identified with his corporate body. When Jesus knocked Paul off his horse on the road to Damascus, he identified himself as "Jesus, whom you are persecuting" (Acts 9:4). Since Jesus had ascended to heaven several years earlier, how could Paul be persecuting *him*? Clearly, he was doing so by persecuting the Church. Jesus apparently considered whatever happened to the Church as happening to *him*. Pain inflicted on his Church is pain inflicted on his body, as much as when spikes were driven into his hands and feet on Calvary.

The call to imitate Jesus is not something people are to carry out by their own efforts. Rather, it's the call to yield to the Spirit and thereby manifest the truth that Christ himself is working in and through us. Christ himself is transforming us into his image.

Christ himself is working through his corporate body to carry on the work he began in his earthly body.

Kingdom people truly constitute a corporate, giant Jesus.

THE BEAUTIFUL REVOLUTION

When people get serious about their call to follow Jesus' example, it's revolutionary. Literally. The Kingdom that Jesus ushered into the world *is* a revolution. It *revolts*. In manifesting the beauty of God's reign, the Kingdom revolts against everything in the world that is inconsistent with this reign.

But the Kingdom revolution is unlike any other the world has known. It's not a revolution of political, nationalistic, or religious ideas and agendas, for Jesus showed no interest in such matters. Indeed, these "revolutions" are trivial by comparison to Christ's, and whenever people have tried to transform the Kingdom into one of these revolutions they have trivialized the Kingdom and denied its essential character.

The revolutions of the world have always been about one group trying to wrest power from another. The revolution Jesus launched, however, is far more radical, for it declares the quest for power over others to be as hopeless as it is sinful. Jesus' Kingdom revolts against this sinful quest for power over others, choosing instead to exercise power *under* others. It's a revolution of humble, self-sacrificial, loving service. It always looks like Jesus, dying on Calvary for the very people who crucified him.

For this reason, the Kingdom doesn't wage war the way people do. It's not like the French or American revolutions, in which people relied on violence to overthrow tyrannical regimes. On the contrary, the Kingdom revolution Jesus unleashed wages war by loving and serving enemies instead of harming and conquering them.

While ordinary revolutions achieve their objectives using the power of the sword, the Kingdom revolution achieves its objectives using the power of the cross. While ordinary revolutions advance by engaging in ugly violence as they sacrifice all who oppose them, the Kingdom revolution advances by manifesting the outrageous beauty of God's love that leads people to sacrifice themselves on behalf of those who oppose them.

The radical Kingdom Jesus embodied and established is all about manifesting the beauty of God's love and revolting against every ugly thing that opposes it.

Christians debate a million complex theological issues. Many are important and legitimate. But from a Kingdom perspective, all those issues are secondary to this one: Are we who profess Christ as Lord imitating his love, service, and sacrifice for others? Are we individually and collectively participating in the beautiful revolution Christ unleashed into the world?[*]

Viva la revolution!

---

[*]At the end of each chapter I strongly encourage readers to go to "What Can We Do? An Action Guide," beginning on p. 175, for suggestions on putting the material of each chapter into practice.

CHAPTER 2

CHRIST
AND CAESAR

For our struggle is not against flesh and blood,
but against ... spiritual forces of evil in the heavenly realms.

EPHESIANS 6:12

THE KINGDOM IS *HOLY*—MEANING "SEPARATE, SET APART, CONSECRATED."
It looks like Jesus, nothing else. We can't simply equate the Kingdom with everything we think is good, noble, and true. Nor can we align the Kingdom with any nation, government, or political ideology. The Kingdom Jesus embodied and established is one of a kind.

When Jesus was on trial, Pilate asked him if he considered himself to be the king of the Jews. Jesus responded, "My kingdom is not of this world. If it were, my servants would fight to prevent my arrest."

Governments and nations have always relied on fighting to survive. They punish criminals who threaten their welfare. They go to war against enemies who attack their borders or stand in the way of their agendas. This is how the kingdoms of the world maintain law and order and advance their causes.

By contrast, the Kingdom that Jesus embodied and established refuses all violence, which is why Jesus pointed to his followers' refusal to fight as proof to Pilate that his kingdom was not of this world. In fact, when Jesus was arrested, one of his followers tried to fight in a kingdom-of-the-world fashion. He pulled out a sword and cut off a guard's ear. Jesus rebuked him and then healed the guard. He was demonstrating that the Kingdom he was establishing doesn't wage war by using violence against enemies but by loving, serving, and healing enemies.

The fact is that no government or nation in history has ever looked remotely like Jesus. None has ever made it a policy *not* to forcefully resist criminals or enemies. None has ever committed itself to blessing criminals, serving enemies, and refusing to retaliate when people or nations do it wrong. Nor has any political regime ever established laws to return evil with good, turn the other cheek, or lend to their enemies without expecting anything in return.

Yet these are what Jesus and his Kingdom are all about.

This isn't meant to be an indictment of the kingdoms of the world, though it's unfortunate that they need to rely on coercive power to keep crime in check and protect their borders. That's the reality of living in a fallen world. Any kingdom that refused to punish criminals and defend itself would quickly fall apart. Scripture indicates that God uses the power of the sword wielded by governments to preserve law and order as much as possible (Romans 13:1–7). Even God, it seems, doesn't expect governments to act "Christian."

Yet this reinforces the point that Jesus' Kingdom looks nothing like the kingdoms of the world, for if God expects anything of Jesus' followers, it's that they act "Christian."

SWORD-POWER VERSUS CROSS-POWER

The difference between the Kingdom of God and the kingdoms of the world comes down to the kind of power they trust.

The kingdoms of the world place their trust in whatever coercive power they can exercise *over* others. We can think of this kind of power as the power of the sword.

In contrast, the Kingdom of God refuses to use coercive power over people, choosing instead to rely exclusively on whatever power it can exercise *under* people. This is the transforming power of humble, self-sacrificial, Christlike love. Exercising power under others is about impacting people's lives by serving them, sacrificing for them, and even being sacrificed by them while refusing to retaliate, as Jesus did. We can think of this kind of power as the *power of the cross*, for the cross is the purest expression of humble, servantlike, self-sacrificial love.

While cross-power may look weak next to sword-power, it is, in fact, the greatest power in the universe. The power of the cross is the only power that can overcome evil rather than merely suppress it for a while. It's the only power that can transform an enemy into a friend. It's the power that God promises will ultimately transform the world. It's the kind of power the omnipotent God himself relied on when he came in the person of Jesus Christ to overcome evil and redeem all of creation from its grip.

KEEPING THE KINGDOM HOLY

Why am I making such a big deal about the different kinds of power manifested by the different kinds of kingdoms? Because the power of the Kingdom of God to attract and transform people lies in its beautiful, humble uniqueness. In a violent world filled with people vying for Caesar-like power *over* others, the Kingdom offers people the peacemaking beauty of Christlike power *under* people.

The power of this distinctive, self-sacrificial beauty is lost, however, whenever the Kingdom of God gets blended with the power-over attitudes and practices of the kingdoms of the world. The Kingdom stops looking like a giant Jesus and starts looking like a giant Caesar—which means the Kingdom for all practical purposes simply ceases to exist.

Kingdom people are called out of the world to be a holy, separate people. We're called to be nonconformists, resisting the "pattern of the world" as we're transformed into the image of Christ. This holy nonconformity isn't just one aspect of who we are—it's the essence of who we are. It's how we manifest the beauty of God's character and Kingdom. Out of the wellspring of the abundant Life we receive from Christ, we are to live in revolt against everything in our own lives, in society, and in the spirit-realm that is inconsistent with God's reign. This can only happen if Jesus followers refuse to get co-opted by other things.

Since everything hangs on keeping the Kingdom holy, it's no surprise that the devil continually tempts Kingdom people to fuse it with the kingdom of the world.

SUCCUMBING TO THE TEMPTATION

It started with Jesus.

The devil offered Jesus all the authority and splendor of the kingdoms of the world, claiming that "it has been given to me, and I can give it to anyone I want to." It was a genuine temptation. Think of all the good things Jesus could have accomplished had he become Caesar over the whole world. He could have immediately put in place all the wisest and most just laws. The painful oppression of his own people could have instantly been brought to an end. He could have ended world hunger. He could have commanded an end to bloodshed around the world.

Jesus came to win all the kingdoms of the world and allevi-ate suffering and oppression. But he didn't come to do it that way. So he resisted the temptation to grab Caesar-like power and chose instead to be faithful to his Father's call to exercise Calvary-like power. He was certainly going to win the kingdoms of the world, but he was going to do it through the slow, impractical, painful route of Calvary.

During the Church's first three centuries, Jesus' followers imitated, for the most part, his beautiful example. They resisted the devil's temptation to grasp power over others, even when it would have been practical for them to do so. Most wouldn't serve in the government or in the military because they believed this was incompatible with a humble, Calvary-like lifestyle. These early Christians kept the kingdom holy by not buying into the values of the empire and by being willing to suffer and even die rather than engage in violent self-defense.

Unfortunately, this came to an abrupt end in the fourth century.

In AD 312 the emperor Constantine allegedly had a vision, which he believed was from God, that told him to fight an important upcoming battle under the banner of the Christ. It was the first time Christ's name was invoked in the cause of violence, but unfortunately it would not be the last.

Constantine won the battle and claimed to become a Christian. He immediately legalized Christianity, and before the end of the century it became the official religion of the Roman empire. For the first time the Church was given access to the power of the sword.

Rather than viewing this new sword-power as Jesus did—that is, as a temptation of the devil that needed to be resisted—influential Church leaders like Eusebius and St. Augustine saw it as a blessing from God! Instead of remaining faithful to the way of the cross, many Church leaders chose to embrace the practical way of the sword. If God has given us Christians the power of the sword, Augustine reasoned, we have a responsibility to use it to advance his cause (as if God's cause could ever be advanced by such means!).

On one level there's nothing new in this line of reasoning. Pagans throughout history have equated military power with divine favor. What was shockingly new, however, is that Jesus' own followers now thought this way.

Once the Church acquired power over others, everything changed. A movement that began by viewing the acquisition of political and military power as a satanic temptation now viewed it as a divine blessing. A movement that was birthed by Christ refusing to conquer his enemies in order to die for them now set out to conquer enemies—for Christ. The faith that previously motivated people to trust in the power of the cross now inspired them to trust in the power of the sword. Those who had previously understood that their job was to serve the world now aspired to rule it. The community that once pointed to their love for enemies and refusal to engage in violence as proof of Christ's lordship now pointed to their ability to violently defeat enemies as proof of Christ's lordship.[1]

In other words, the movement that had previously suffered

because it refused to buy into the nationalistic ideology of the empire was now, to a large degree, defined by the ideology of that empire. The Church allowed itself to become co-opted by typical, pagan nationalism. The beautiful revolution begun by Jesus was largely reduced to an ugly, violent-tending, nationalistic religion.

This is the religion of Christendom, the Church "militant and triumphant." Insofar as it looked and acted like a religious version of Caesar, it was as far removed from the Kingdom as any religion could be. For the Kingdom always looks like Jesus, not Caesar.

RETURNING TO THE EXAMPLE OF JESUS

Jesus was born in politically hot times. The Jews of his day were deeply divided over, among other issues, how they should respond to the oppressive Roman government that ruled them. Time after time people tried to get Jesus to weigh in on one side or the other. But Jesus always refused.

For instance, when one man tried to get Jesus to side with him on what he thought was an unjust inheritance law, Jesus basically said, "Who made me your lawyer?" When the crowd tried to elicit Jesus' opinion on the divisive issue of taxes, Jesus in essence said, "Why should we who bear the image of God fight over what to do with coins that bear the image of Caesar? The only thing we should worry about is giving God everything that bears his image — namely, our whole self."[2]

Jesus refused to let the Kingdom he came to establish get fused with the political squabbles of his day. He never so much as commented on the pagan political leadership of his day, despite the fact that they often acted in cruel and perverse ways. Not only this, but Jesus invited both Simon, a zealot, and Matthew, a tax collector, to be his disciples. Though zealots and tax collectors were at opposite ends of the political spectrum, Jesus never mentioned this difference. It shows that even the most extreme political differences between people are rendered inconsequential whenever people belong to the Kingdom Jesus established. For Jesus' Kingdom, again, is "not of this world."

Jesus kept the Kingdom holy by how he lived, and we are called to do the same.

At the same time, every aspect of Jesus' life—including his death—confronted some aspect of the *polis* (Greek for "society") and was in this sense political. In fact, while Jesus didn't utter a word about politics, he was a subversive political revolutionary. His life, ministry, teachings, death, and resurrection revolted against every unjust and oppressive aspect of the *polis*. This is why Jesus was a threat to the religious and political authorities—and ultimately why they felt they had to crucify him.

We who have pledged our lives to following Jesus are to be political revolutionaries in this same way. Rather than putting our trust in how we vote every couple years, we're to follow Jesus' example and vote with our lives, day in and day out.

Following Jesus gives us no special wisdom on how to resolve complex political issues—issues that divide the *polis*. On these matters Christians are on the same footing as others. But if our pledge to follow Christ means anything, it means we have a unique willingness to individually and collectively sacrifice our own time and resources to serve people afflicted by the divisions in our society.

For example, following Jesus gives us no special wisdom about what the government should do about poverty. Intelligent, caring people can and do disagree on this. But our pledge to follow Jesus must make us willing to sacrificially care for the poor—because this is what Jesus did. Nor does following Jesus give us any special wisdom about when and how government should use violence against those it regards as a threat to its well-being. But our pledge to follow Jesus must make us willing to love and serve those who threaten our well-being rather than use violence against them.

Jesus followers aren't to posture themselves as Caesar's wise advisors, for Jesus never did this. Some claim the Church is supposed to be "the conscience of government," but there's absolutely no basis for this claim in the New Testament. Rather, we're to position ourselves as society's humble servants, for this is what Jesus did. Our sole responsibility as Kingdom people is to live the way Jesus lived and revolt the way Jesus revolted. Every aspect of our life is to manifest the revolting beauty Jesus manifested.

If a significant portion of Jesus followers lived like this, the Church might actually become "the conscience of government" in the sense that our contrasting lifestyle would draw attention to the injustices of the state. Our service to the poor would expose government's lack of concern, and our ability to break cycles of violence by loving enemies would expose the folly of government's reliance on violence.

Sadly, the Church has failed so miserably at displaying its unique power to transform society that most Christians today can't even imagine this happening. The only kind of power they see accomplishing anything is Caesar's. So instead of working together to do what Jesus did, we often waste time fighting each other over what Caesar should do.

THE DANGER OF POLITICS

Does this mean that Jesus followers should never participate in government? Not necessarily.

Certainly followers of Jesus aren't to think we have a duty to participate in government. Our one Lord is Jesus Christ and our sole duty is to him and the Kingdom he came to establish. We cannot serve two masters. Our Lord commands us to submit to government, insofar as this is possible, and to pray for our leaders so that peace and justice may reign as much as possible. These are the only "duties" Jesus followers have toward government, and we only have these because God requires them of us, not because we owe government anything.

Along the same lines, it's clear from the New Testament that Jesus followers aren't to place any hope or trust in any government. We might at times approve of a particular person or policy in government, thinking they will be good for society. But we must always remember that Satan "controls the entire world" (1 John 5:19) and owns the authority of all governments (Luke 4:5–7)—including the ones we approve of. And we must always remember that governments and militaries are "less than nothing" to our sovereign God (Isaiah 40:15, 17) and are all destined to pass away when the loving reign of God is fully established on earth.

Having said this, I cannot concur with those who go further and argue that we have a duty *not* to participate in government. Paul didn't hesitate to humbly speak to political authorities and take full advantage of his rights as a Roman citizen when it made sense to do so (Acts 21:37–39; 22:25–30). He obviously wasn't expressing any trust in the Roman government to bring about the Kingdom. Nor was he trying to fix the governmental system of his day. But he was taking advantage of some say-so that he had as a Roman citizen. In democratic societies we get asked our opinion of how the society should be run, and I see no reason why one can't give it, if they feel called to do so.[3]

In fact, while most political issues are ambiguous enough for decent and intelligent people to disagree about, there are exceptional circumstances that arise from time to time that require all decent people—and therefore Kingdom people—to confront unambiguous evil by all means possible, including affecting the political process. One thinks, for example, of the rise of Nazism in Germany, of apartheid in America and South Africa, and of the ongoing child-sex slave trade in eastern Asia and elsewhere. To refrain from using *every* means available to confront unambiguous evil on the grounds that there is no precedent for it in the ministry of Jesus is pedantic and against the spirit of the New Testament.

Yet even with unambiguous situations such as these, followers of Jesus need to take great care to preserve their distinctive Kingdom perspective and lifestyle. We must always be on guard against the seductive lure of the "power-over" regime—and we must never compromise our call to love our enemies.

Whatever limited good we can accomplish by political means, we must remember that the hope of the world doesn't reside here.

It resides in God using surrendered people to usher in his Kingdom through self-sacrificial acts of love. Our focus must not be on resolving political conflicts but on individually and collectively looking like Jesus. Our sole confidence must be in God who uses the foolishness of our self-sacrificial love to bring about his Kingdom — which, let us never forget, is "not of this world."

THE REIGN OF THE POWERS

The Kingdom is "not of this world," and neither is its warfare. Jews had always believed that God confronted spiritual opposition in carrying out his will on earth. In the Old Testament these evil forces were usually depicted as cosmic monsters and hostile waters that threatened the earth.[4] For a variety of reasons this belief in spiritual warfare intensified significantly in the two centuries leading up to Christ. Many Jews came to believe the earth was largely under the control of evil forces. Many also believed that in the near future God was going to bring this demonic oppression to an end by breaking into world history, freeing Israel, and liberating creation. This intensified understanding of evil and this new view of history is commonly referred to as the "apocalyptic" worldview.[5]

There's no question that Jesus and the revolution he inaugurated were steeped in this apocalyptic worldview. This is evident throughout the New Testament. The unprecedented authority ascribed to Satan, the frequent depictions of illnesses and deformities as demonically caused, and the general characterization of this present epoch as evil and as approaching its end all reflect this worldview.[6]

Most important for our purposes, however, is the way the New Testament reflects an apocalyptic worldview in speaking about evil. We find references to Satan, rulers, principalities, powers, and authorities, along with dominions, cosmic powers, thrones, spiritual forces, elemental spirits of the universe, gods, and a number of other spiritual entities. For the sake of brevity I'll refer to this entire realm of cosmic forces simply as "the Powers."[7]

Understanding this dimension of the apocalyptic worldview considerably deepens our understanding of the revolution Jesus inaugurated, for it means that Jesus' radically countercultural ministry wasn't first and foremost a form of social and political protest, though it certainly was that. It was, rather, most fundamentally a form of spiritual warfare.

If understood in its original apocalyptic context, it's apparent that Jesus' deliverance ministry wasn't the only way Jesus confronted evil. Every aspect of the Kingdom of God Jesus manifested revolted against a corresponding aspect of the kingdom of the Powers. In Jesus, and in the movement he came to establish, the long expected apocalyptic battle between God and the Powers was—and still is—being waged.

When Jesus revolted against the oppressive religion of his day, for example, he was engaging in warfare against the Powers that use religion to oppress people. So too, when Jesus refused to live in accordance with his culture's assumptions, laws, and social taboos regarding nationalism, race, gender, class, and wealth, he wasn't just waging a social protest; he was engaging in warfare against the Powers that oppress people by empowering these things.

Paul reflects this point when he informs us that "our struggle is not against flesh and blood, but against the rulers, against the authorities, against the powers of this dark world and against the spiritual forces of evil in the heavenly realms." From a Kingdom perspective, if it's got "flesh and blood"—if it's human—it's not our enemy. To the contrary, if it's got "flesh and blood" it's someone we're commanded to love and thus someone we're to be fighting *for*—even if they regard us as their enemy.

We may profoundly disagree with their political, ethical, and religious views. We may find their lifestyle disgusting. They may in fact be criminals that need to be locked up behind bars. They may threaten us and our nation. Still, from a Kingdom perspective, our struggle is never against other humans. Our struggle is rather *for* them and *against* the evil that works to oppress both them and us.

The primary way we wage war on behalf of others, including

our enemies, is by imitating Jesus and refusing to buy into any aspect of the Powers' oppressive regime—including the universal tendency to make other people our enemies. Whereas earthly wars are fought with pride, strength, and violence, the Kingdom war is fought in humility, weakness, and love. Any aspect of our own life, our society, or our global community that is under the Powers' influence and is inconsistent with the loving reign of God as revealed in Jesus is something that we are called to revolt against.

BEING THE KINGDOM

Gandhi once said, "Be the change you want to see in the world." Though Gandhi didn't consider himself a Christian, he was here advocating a profound Kingdom truth.

Often people want to change the world before they themselves are changed. It never works. In fact, I'd argue that nothing damages the world more than damaged people constantly trying to fix it. The best thing anyone can do for the world is to follow Gandhi's advice and simply *be* the change they want to see in the world.

Our job as Kingdom people is not to fix government, society, and the world. Our job is not to position ourselves as Caesar's wise and morally superior advisors. Our job is not to come up with the smartest, most practical, most caring solutions to the world's problems. As individuals and as a tribe, our job is simply to *be* the Kingdom. Our job is simply to *be* the change God wants to see in the world. Our job is simply to *be* faithful, however impractical and irresponsible this may look to people who put all their trust in the power-over efficiency of laws, policies, technology, bombs, and bullets.

This is our call. This is our identity. And this is our warfare. To live faithful to the reign of God is to live in revolt against everything that is inconsistent with this reign. To be conformed to the will of God is to revolt against the Powers' pull to conform to their ways.

This is the revolution of beautiful servant-love Christ unleashed into the world.

In the chapters that follow we will explore twelve beautiful aspects of Jesus' life that represent the heart of this revolution and that revolt against twelve ugly aspects of the world under the oppression of the Powers.

Viva la revolution!

CHAPTER 3

THE REVOLT
AGAINST IDOLATRY

Dear children, keep yourselves from idols.

1 JOHN 5:21

Everybody's got a hungry heart ...

BRUCE SPRINGSTEEN

CONFESSIONS OF A BEWILDERED DEMON CHILD

I wasn't the best kid growing up. Actually, I was pretty terrible. I suspect I had what they today would label a "behavioral disorder." I have a pretty good alibi though. Really. My mom died of leukemia when I was two, and, I'm told, I never seemed to get over it. After my mom died, my dad often traveled for weeks at a time, leaving my grandmother to raise me and my siblings while he was gone. I was hyperactive. She was old and cranky. It didn't go well.

In first grade my dad and stepmother sent me to a very strict Catholic school, which only seemed to make things worse. Back then nuns didn't use fancy words like "behavioral disorder" or "hyperactive." Kids like me were just plain possessed, and the nuns had ways of kicking the demon out of you. At that time nuns could still use "corporeal punishment" (translation: "beat the crap out of you")—and they did. (I suspect the chronic soreness in my neck and back to this day is at least partly due to being repeatedly whacked on the head with a huge Bible.)

I would regularly be sent to the Mother Superior's office—the head nun who had the temperament of a starving pit bull and the build of a young Arnold Schwarzenegger. She would ask me why I did what I did, and I would always mutter back, "I don't know."

This only made her more angry, but I was telling the truth. I had no clue why I put tacks on teachers' chairs, pulled girls' hair, threw spit balls, and made farting noises. Fast forward to eighth grade and I still had no clue why I started a massive food fight during lunch, why I picked fights with tough guys, or why I helped set a science teacher on fire.

Since then, I've come to realize that most don't *really* know why they do what they do. They may have great psychological insights into themselves, and these may all be accurate. But I don't think most people have any more idea than I did as to what drives them at the core of their being.

THE HUNGRY HEART

To begin to get at what drives us at the core of our being, see if you can discern what all the following behaviors have in common.

- A couple with two kids purchases a bigger and more luxurious house than they need, even though it means they'll both have to work more and see each other and the kids less.
- A Hindu woman prays to a shrine of Vishnu three times a day.
- Despite failing health, one of the world's 950 or so billionaires continues to work fifteen or more hours a day and rarely takes vacations.
- A middle-aged man leaves his wife of twenty years to move in with a woman half his age. He also starts smoking cigarettes and driving a Harley.
- A perfectly normal-looking middle-aged woman spends a year's salary on breast implants, a face lift, a tummy-tuck, and thigh reductions. She then becomes unsatisfied with the size of her lips and nose.
- A "Christian" group carries signs like "God hates fags" as they picket the military burial of a gay Marine.

- Despite having a sexually transmitted disease, a young woman compulsively engages in sexual intercourse with virtual strangers on a regular basis.
- One teen stabs another at school in retaliation for being publicly insulted.
- A pastor habitually gossips about others.
- A husband and father puts his family in financial distress by continuing to pursue his gambling addiction behind their backs.
- An eighth grader splashes a flammable liquid on a science teacher, knowing full well his friend has matches and is crazy enough to use them in just such a situation.

Do you see the common denominator?

While there's always a multitude of psychological and social reasons why people do what they do, I submit that there's one driving motivation shared by all these people.

Bruce Springsteen got it right: "Everybody's got a hungry heart."

The hunger Springsteen is talking about goes to the core of our being. It's a hunger not just to survive, but to feel fully alive. It's a hunger to experience fullness of worth, significance, and security. It's a hunger to have what I'm calling "Life." It's the kind of Life Jesus incarnated and came to share with us. It lies at the heart of all that the Kingdom is about.

"I have come that they may have life," he said, "and have it to the full" (John 10:10).

As I look back on my youth, I now see that, more than anything else, I was trying to feel like I had worth. When I did outrageous things, I felt more alive than when I conformed to social expectations. I needed a certain group of peers to look up to me. I needed to stand out. I needed to feel significant and special. Unfortunately, my willingness to push the envelope was the only unique way I could come up with at the time. (I actually remember feeling jealous once when another student got in more trouble than I did.)

The teen who stabs a peer is operating out of this same belief, which is why he felt his source of Life was threatened by an insult. The pastor who habitually gossips operates out of the same belief.

The couple who purchases a bigger house than they need is operating out of an unconscious belief that their worth is defined by their possessions and the appearance of success. So is the billionaire who, despite already having more money than he could possibly spend, continues to sacrifice health and relationships to make more. It's the same story for the man who continues to risk his family's financial future through his gambling obsession.

The Hindu who prays to Vishnu is operating out of a belief that her worth is associated with pleasing a particular god. So are the Christians who maliciously picket a gay Marine's funeral.

The middle-aged man who leaves his wife for a younger woman is operating out of an unconscious belief that his worth is linked to feeling young and sexually attractive—at least more so than it is to remaining faithful to his marriage vows. The woman who spends all her money on cosmetic surgery is operating out of this same belief, as is the person who compulsively engages in indiscriminant sexual activity.

Why do we do what we do? There are a million, perfectly valid, social and psychological explanations. Despite the fact that few are aware of it, however, the most fundamental explanation is that we're all trying to feel fully alive.

Everybody's got a hungry heart. Everybody's trying to feel fully alive. Everybody craves Life.

THE HUNGRY GOD

There's nothing wrong with wanting to feel fully alive. It's a central part of what makes us human. Animals are content with mere biological life, but humans never are. We need more.

We're supposed to experience a fullness of worth because, as a matter of fact, we have inestimable worth. We crave real Life because God created us to experience real Life.

Only God himself can satisfy this hunger. It's true, of course, that we can and should find some fulfillment in our relationships, accomplishments, and certain profound experiences (of music, nature, art, and so on). But if we're at all self-aware, we know that even in the best relationships, the greatest accomplishments, and the most profound experiences, something is missing.

Like the proverbial splinter in the brain that Morpheus talks about in the film *The Matrix*, we're nagged by a certain sense of emptiness. And the reason is that, at the core of our being, we hunger for more. We hunger for a depth of Life only God can give.

Why would God create us with this insatiable hunger? The answer is that he wants to feed us — with himself.

God made us desperately hungry for him because he, out of love, is hungry for us. His hunger for us isn't an expression of neediness or emptiness, as is our hunger for him. Rather, his hunger for us is an expression of the fullness of his perfect love. Precisely because he is a God of perfect love, he creates beings with whom he deeply wants to share himself and who desperately need him. Our in-built, insatiable hunger is simply God's loving way of drawing us into a beautiful, eternal relationship with himself.

If you doubt that God yearns to be in a love relationship with you, just look at what he did to pave the way for it to happen. In Jesus, the almighty God set aside the glory of heaven, became a human, took upon himself the hellish consequences of our sin, and died an agonizing death on the cross.

If that doesn't strike you as the behavior of a desperate lover, what would?

Jesus dying on the cross reveals the beauty of the lovingly hungry God.

A WORLD OF POTENTIAL IDOLS

God creates us with a hunger only he can satisfy, but this hunger doesn't force us to enter into a relationship with him. Love can't be coerced. If we choose, we can try to satisfy our hunger in other ways.

From its opening chapter, the Bible is the story of humanity's futile attempt to find Life outside of God. This is what the story of Adam and Eve is about. Under the influence of the serpent, Eve embraced a deceptive, untrustworthy picture of God that caused her to stop trusting God as her source of Life. As a result, Eve was led to believe she could acquire Life on her own. She was deceived into thinking that the forbidden tree could give her something she thought she needed.

This isn't just a story of something that happened "once upon a time." It's the story of every one of us. Instead of relying on God to meet our needs, we try to meet them on our own. We all eat of the forbidden tree. (In the next chapter we'll find out why its mysteriously called "the Tree of the Knowledge of Good and Evil.")

The Bible calls this idolatry. Most westerners think that idolatry is about people worshiping a statue of Vishnu or Buddha or some other divinity. But the truth is that an idol is anything we treat as a god; that is, anything we use to satisfy the hunger in our soul that only our Creator can satisfy. An idol is anything other than God that we rely on as a source of Life.

Historically, many people have tried to get Life from religious idols. Religious idolaters attempt to get Life from whatever mistaken picture of God they happen to embrace — including the mistaken idea that divinity can be found in or through physical objects (such as a statue of Vishnu or Buddha). The ultimate worth of religious idolaters is rooted in the religious activities they do or religious doctrines they believe, both of which they think please their gods. Even when Christians try to get Life from (what they assume is) the rightness of their behaviors and beliefs instead of from God himself, they are guilty of idolatry.

But there are as many nonreligious idols as religious ones. In Western culture, sex, wealth, and power are the most common idols. But others make idols of their nation, race, talents, looks, or fame. In fact, just about everything in this world is a potential idol, for just about anything can be used as a means of trying to feel fully alive.

THE MISERABLE FEEDING FRENZY

When the thing that makes you feel fully alive is something as iffy as sexual vigor, wealth, or power, it wreaks havoc on your soul. On some level you know that you may never attain the sexual experiences, wealth, or power you're striving for.

Even if you manage to get what you're seeking, you know that it's just a matter of time before you lose it. There's a multitude of competitors for the wealth, power, and fame you've acquired, and at some moment they might gain an advantage over you. And even if you manage to stay on top of the hill, you know that you're slowly going to waste away and die. Aging and death are never kind to idols.

Not only this, but even if you're successful at acquiring all the worth you can from your sexuality, wealth, power—or whatever idols you happen to embrace—you know it doesn't even satisfy you while you enjoy them. We can distract ourselves from our inner emptiness but it never goes away.

The Bible describes living this way—which Paul calls "the flesh" —as a miserable affair. Life in "the flesh" is full of anxiety, hopelessness, envy, strife, anger, and bitterness. The idolatrous world of "the flesh" is a competitive feeding frenzy of desperately hungry people trying to scarf up a morsel of fleeting worth from a limited number of idolatrous sources. Idolatry is at the root of most of the misery in the world.

Trace your own despair, anxiety, or bitterness back far enough and, more likely than not, you'll discover there's something other than God that you're clinging to as a source of Life.

Not only this, but throughout history idolatry has been at the root of all the hatred, conflict, and bloodshed in the world. People will kill to acquire and protect their source of feeling fully alive and worthwhile. Idolatry and violence go hand-in-hand.

THE BEAUTIFUL TRUTH ABOUT GOD—AND US

Jesus came into this oppressed, idolatrous world to reintroduce us to the true source of Life and thereby rescue us from this futile, miserable, idolatrous feeding frenzy. The reason he can do this is because he reveals who God truly is—and who we truly are.

In contrast to the pathetic picture of God that the serpent gave to Eve, Jesus reveals the true character of God. This is why the New Testament refers to Jesus as the Word, Image, and perfect expression of God. It's why Jesus himself insisted that if we see him, we see God the Father. And it's why the New Testament repeatedly encourages us to fix our spiritual eyes on Jesus. The outrageous love and mercy displayed throughout Jesus' life, and especially in his death, is the love and mercy of God himself.

If we are willing to trust him, Jesus frees us from the bondage of the enemy's deceptive picture of God. He frees us to return to God as our one and only source of Life.

At the same time, Jesus confronts the lie that there's something humans need to do, and can do, to acquire Life on our own. The fact that God himself became a human and died for our sin reveals that we can't find Life on our own. If we had the ability to save ourselves, it wouldn't have been necessary for God to go to this radical extreme to save us. But the fact that God did this out of love reveals we don't need to try to find Life on our own. Jesus reveals that, despite our sin, God remained desperately in love with us and as a result opened up the way for us to enter into the eternal relationship with him that he's always wanted.

In Jesus we discover the beauty of the true God and the beauty of what he created and saved us to be. In Jesus we discover the unsurpassable and unconditional worth, significance, and security our hearts were created to enjoy. In Jesus, our hearts finally find what they've been hungry for, so we are empowered to break our miserable addiction to idols.

FREEDOM

A "kingdom," as I wrote earlier, is a king's domain. To belong to the Kingdom of God means we surrender our life to God and make it part of the domain over which he rules. When we do this, we immediately begin to experience the Life that comes from God and begin to be transformed into the image of Jesus.

Just as the Jesus-looking Kingdom begins as a mustard seed and slowly grows to take over the whole earth, so the Kingdom begins as a mustard seed in our own life and gradually grows to take over our entire existence. We become citizens of the Kingdom the moment we genuinely surrender our lives, but we experience and manifest the true Life of the Kingdom only as we learn to yield to him on a daily basis.

As the Kingdom grows in us, our addiction to idols wanes. As we grow in our capacity to experience the true God and our true worth in Jesus Christ, we increasingly find that the idols of the world lose their power—and even their appeal. When a person truly experiences their unsurpassable worth as a child of the King, what could all the wealth, power, sex, or fame in the world possibly offer? Nothing.

Jesus said we shall know the truth and the truth shall set us free. This is the freedom he was talking about. To the extent that our longing for worth, significance, and security is fully satisfied by our relationship with Christ, we crave nothing and fear nothing. We are literally a people who have nothing to gain and nothing to lose. Having lost our life, we've found true Life. This is true freedom!

This freedom is what empowers Jesus followers to imitate his radically self-sacrificial lifestyle. While others live out of a center of emptiness that forces them to strive to acquire and protect their idolatrous sources of Life, Kingdom people live out of a center of fullness that frees them to live with abandon as they focus on carrying out God's will "on earth as it is in heaven."

This is the heart of the Kingdom revolution Jesus unleashed in the world. It manifests the beauty of God's free Life while revolting against the ugliness of idolatrous bondage.

Viva la revolution!

CHAPTER 4

THE REVOLT
AGAINST JUDGMENT

A man cannot raise himself up above any other man
or set himself before him as a model,
for he knows himself to be the greatest of all sinners.
He can excuse the sin of another, but never his own.

DIETRICH BONHOEFFER

WAKING UP TO MENTAL GOSSIP

About ten years ago I was shopping in a mall with my wife, Shelley. Now, I don't know if this is a male-female thing, or if it's unique to Shelley and me, but shopping tends to excite her while it makes me profoundly tired. As soon as I walk into a store—unless it's a bookstore or a drum shop (I *love* drums!)—I get sleepy. So, as usual, Shelley ended up going from store to store while I parked my tired behind on a bench in the center of the mall.

For about ten minutes I just watched people. Then suddenly, as if someone had placed a megaphone to my thoughts, I heard my own running commentary about almost everyone and everything I saw. Much of it was positive, but some of it was, frankly, complete trash. I heard myself say things like:

"What kind of parent would treat a child like *that?*"
"Could her dress make it more obvious what she wants guys
    to notice?"
"Definitely gay."
"What a nag."
"Ohhh. Tough guy aren't we?"
"Like that person *needs* that Big Mac."

It was like I was gossiping in the privacy of my brain. I was surprised by this since I've always thought of myself as a tolerant, nonjudgmental person.

When I started paying attention, I found that in most cases the person I watched triggered an association in my mind. For example, something about the lady I judged to be a "nag" reminded me of the stepmother who raised me.

But beneath these psychological reasons I discovered an even deeper motivation for my internal gossip: I was engaging in mental gossip because it gave me a heightened sense of worth. Contrasting myself with others made me feel more fully alive. I was trying to get Life from an idol, and the idol was my judgment of others. The motivation was profoundly subtle, which is why I'd never noticed it before. But once I woke up to it, it was undeniable.

Like all judgment, my mental gossip was predicated on the assumption that I am qualified to be the insightful arbiter of other people's parenting skills, dressing styles, sexual orientation, dietary habits, and the like. It presupposed my superiority. However imperfect I may be, at least I wasn't like *that* person. And though I was unconscious of it before then, on some level this private judgment game made me feel significant.

Some might think I'm making a mountain out of a molehill. After all, I didn't actually verbalize my thoughts to anyone, so was I *really* judging them? And doesn't everybody think like this at times? Sure, having private judgments may not be ideal and, technically speaking, may even be sinful—but it's surely not a serious sin. What's the big deal?

This *is* a big deal. The fact that everybody does it, and that we tend to minimize it, simply demonstrates how serious a problem this is and how hard it is to confront.

JUDGMENT AND DISCERNMENT

First, we need to be clear about what "judgment" is and what it is not.

On the one hand, Jesus and the New Testament writers repeatedly and emphatically forbid us to judge others. On the other hand, we're repeatedly and emphatically told we can, for example, know a tree by its fruits. Doesn't that involve judgment? We're also instructed to grow in our ability to distinguish between good and evil, and we're told to hold one another accountable. In fact, in cases where a brother or sister will not turn from a seriously harmful behavior, we're told to remove them from our fellowship. Don't these instructions involve judging people?

The answer is *no*, not in the sense that I am using the term — and here's why. The Greek word usually translated "judgment" is *krino*. We get the word "critic" from this word, and it literally means "to cut, divide, or separate things." A movie critic, for example, is one who helps us separate good movies from bad ones.

Now there's a kind of separating (*krino*) that is appropriate and necessary, and a kind of separating that is utterly inappropriate and sinful. For the sake of clarity I'll label the good kind *discernment* and the bad kind *judgment*. Every day we need to discern whether certain things are helpful or unhelpful, godly or ungodly, wise or stupid. We need to continually discern the difference between a good use of time and money and a bad use of time and money. We need to discern whether we're safe or in danger, whether we think its going to rain or not, whether we think a person should be hired for a job or not, whether it's wise to trust a person or not, whether we look better in the blue dress or the hot pink one, whether we agree with an author or not, and a million things of this sort. This sort of discernment is obviously good and natural. We couldn't live without making such practical distinctions.

This sort of discernment obviously is not what Jesus and New Testament authors are talking about when they forbid us to "judge." For when we judge, as I was doing in the mall that afternoon, we aren't distinguishing between things. We're rather separating ourselves from other people and placing ourselves (or "our" group) above them. We're contrasting ourselves favorably with others as a way of making ourselves feel more worthy, more significant, or more secure.

Despite the fact that Christians tend to minimize the sin of judging (in fact, many seem to specialize in it), this *is* a big deal! In fact, not only is judgment a form of idolatry, it's the most fundamental form of idolatry there is. It's why the forbidden tree in the garden that brought about the Fall of humanity was called "the Tree of the Knowledge of Good and Evil." When we reject God as our sole source of Life, we invariably try to acquire Life by pretending we're God and judging others. This is the foundational sin in the Bible, because it blocks the foundational command in the Bible, which is to love God, ourselves, and others.[1]

Judgment *is* a big deal!

JUDGMENT AND IDOLATRY

Not only is judging a form of idolatry, it's involved in all other forms of idolatry. Every idol contains a particular version of the Tree of the Knowledge of Good and Evil.

Here's an illustration.

Throughout history most people have found some element of their core worth, significance, and security in their national identity. They are certain that the things their country values are also the things that "God" (or "the gods") values. Consequently, most have been naively certain that whatever furthers the interests of their nation is good while whatever hinders or threatens the interests of their nation is evil.

Since the interests and values of nations frequently conflict, human history is largely a macabre river of blood, supplied by people killing and being killed for their nations. And they've almost always done so in the name of defending "the good" (their nation, their god) against a threatening "evil" (the opposing nations and gods).

While some wars may be more justified than others, what drives the whole enterprise is that people embrace differing nationalistic idols and thus differing versions of the Knowledge of Good and Evil. People on both sides whose source of Life is wrapped up with their patriotism just *know* that they happened to be born on the side of the good, while their enemy happened to be born on the side of evil.

In America, for example, most people (including, it seems, most Christians) just *know* that God is on the side of political freedom and that it is worth killing for—despite Jesus' command that his followers are to love and do good to all enemies, and despite the fact that neither Jesus nor anyone else in the Bible ever said a word about political freedom.

The same thing can happen with religion for religious people, race for racists, political parties for the politically minded, and sports teams for overzealous sports enthusiasts (hence the occasional bloody riots at soccer matches). Whatever advances and protects our particular idolatrous source of Life is "good" while whatever hinders or threatens our particular idolatrous source of Life is "evil."

The same thing is true for a million other idols. If a person's source of Life is sex, whatever affirms, advances, and protects their sexual vibrancy is "good," while whatever negates, hinders, or threatens it is "evil." If wealth is a person's idol, whatever advances or protects their money and possessions is "good," while whatever hinders or threatens those things is "evil." So it is with the idols of power, fame, intelligence, achievements, or any other idol you can imagine.

The kid in second grade who stole my show by getting into more trouble than I did was, in that moment, an "evil" to me, for he detracted from my twisted, juvenile, idolatrous source of Life.

Of course, only in certain circumstances do we explicitly think of our competitors in the idolatrous feeding frenzy as technically "evil." More frequently we identify them merely as bad or stupid or losers or greedy or by some other derogatory term. But however we think of them—and *this is the crucial point*—we are detracting from their God-given dignity and worth by the way we think, speak, and respond to them. And to this extent, we are not agreeing with God that they have unsurpassable worth as evidenced by the fact that Jesus died for them. We are not self-sacrificially loving them as Jesus called us to. Instead, we are rebelling against God and judging them. We are eating from our particular version of "the Tree of the Knowledge of Good and Evil."

RECEIVING AND ASCRIBING UNSURPASSABLE WORTH

Judgment is the foundational sin in the Bible because it prevents us from obeying the foundational command in the Bible, which is to love others the way God loves us. To fully appreciate why judgment is so heinous, therefore, we need to explore why love is so important.

People today have a lot of screwy ideas about what love is. Part of the problem is that we use the word *love* to cover everything from sexual intercourse ("making love") to pets ("I *love* my cat") to hairstyles ("I just *love* your hair"). No wonder we're confused.

The Bible gives us a profoundly simple and beautiful definition of love. The Bible uses the word *agape*—the most important kind of love there is. This is the love God has for us and that we're supposed to apply to ourselves and extend to others. The Bible defines this kind of love by pointing us to Jesus Christ.

"This is how we know what love is," John says. "Jesus Christ laid down his life for us. And we ought to lay down our lives for one another" (1 John 3:16).

God expressed his opinion of our worth by becoming a human and laying down his life for us. *This*, John says, is love. It is about expressing the worth of another by what you're willing to sacrifice for them. It's about ascribing worth to another at cost to yourself when necessary. In fact, real love, as defined by Jesus, is about expressing the *unsurpassable* worth of another by being willing to sacrifice *everything* for them.

As we saw in the last chapter, God created us with a desperate need to receive and experience this kind of unsurpassable worth.

But God also created us to express this kind of perfect love and therefore ascribe to others this kind of unsurpassable worth. Having our innermost hunger satisfied with the unsurpassable love and worth that comes from the one true source of Life, we are to extend this same love and worth to others.

This is why John adds "we ought to lay down our lives for one another." We are to love all others the way God loves us. As God ascribes unsurpassable worth to us, despite our sin, we are to ascribe unsurpassable worth to others, despite their sin.

This is the central defining mark of the Kingdom. Whatever else is implied in acknowledging God as King, at the very least it implies that we commit to agreeing with God's opinion about what people are worth. And he expressed this opinion on Calvary.

Our most fundamental job as Kingdom people, therefore, is to express to all people at all times our agreement with God that they have unsurpassable worth. And we are to express this by our willingness to make sacrifices and, if necessary, be sacrificed on their behalf.

Insofar as we do this, and *only* insofar as we do this, we look like Jesus and manifest the beauty of the domain over which God reigns.

THIS IS WHAT THE KINGDOM IS ALL ABOUT

Nothing is more central to the Kingdom than agreeing with God about every person's unsurpassable worth and reflecting this in how we act toward them. Nothing is more important than living in Christlike love for all people at all times. In fact, compared to love, nothing else really matters in the Kingdom.

In 1 Corinthians 13 Paul says that all the most impressive religious and humanitarian activity in the world is completely worthless, except insofar as it expresses love.

A person may speak in tongues—even the glorious tongues of angels—but if his speaking isn't motivated by love, it's just religious noise.

A person may have the gift of prophecy and be able to proclaim the word of God in ways that dazzle audiences and build incredible megachurches. But if the use of these gifts isn't motivated by love, they are, from a Kingdom perspective, utterly worthless.

It doesn't make the least bit of difference that a person has breathtaking insight into all mysteries or that they possess all knowledge. This would undoubtedly impress crowds and maybe even get them on the cover of *Christianity Today*, but if their activity isn't motivated by a desire to ascribe unsurpassable worth to all people at all times, it's meaningless.

Nor does it matter that a person has faith such that they can command mountains to be relocated and the mountains actually obey. This sort of miracle-working ability would certainly land them a nice spot on Christian television and would undoubtedly make them an excellent fund-raiser. But, according to Paul, it's completely devoid of value unless it's fueled by an agreement with God that every person alive was worth God himself dying for.

Finally, and perhaps most surprising, even if a person gives every single thing they own to the poor and endures great hardships in the course of their ministry, if their actions aren't motivated by a love that looks like Jesus dying on the cross, it accomplishes absolutely nothing.

Love, clearly, is the all-or-nothing of Kingdom living. The "only thing that counts," Paul says, "is faith expressing itself through love." We are to "do everything in love," he says. Love is the primary expression of Kingdom Life. Where God truly reigns in an individual or community, they will look like Jesus, sacrificially ascribing unsurpassable worth to all people, no ifs, ands, or buts.

REVOLTING AGAINST JUDGMENT

Judgment and life in the Kingdom are antithetical to each other. It's impossible to ascribe unsurpassable worth to another while we're detracting worth from another.

Every single judgmental thought I had toward others as I sat in the mall that day prevented me from doing the one thing I was supposed to be doing as a Kingdom person. Instead of getting my whole worth from God, I was trying to get worth from the idol of my judgment. And instead of submitting to God and agreeing with him that every person I saw had unsurpassable worth, I was rebelliously disagreeing with him and detracting worth from others to idolatrously ascribe worth to myself.

Jesus came to free us from idols and restore us to the Life God intends for us. He thus came to free us from judgment and restore our capacity to love the way God loves us.

To help us get free, Jesus and the rest of the New Testament emphasize the importance of revolting against judgment. In one crucial passage, Jesus says: "Do not judge, or you too will be judged. For in the same way you judge others, you will be judged, and with the measure you use, it will be measured to you" (Matthew 7:2).

This is a truly remarkable teaching. Jesus is teaching us that we can either play the judgment game or the grace game. If you don't want to be judged, he says, don't judge others. Extend to them the same gracious love that God has extended to you. But if you insist on playing the judgment game, then know that the judgment you give is the judgment you'll get.

We simply can't eat from the Tree of Life and the Tree of the Knowledge of Good and Evil at the same time. We can't love like God loves while trying to judge like only God can judge.

This teaching becomes even more remarkable when Jesus goes on to say, "Why do you look at the speck of sawdust in someone else's eye and pay no attention to the plank in your own eye? How can you say, 'Let me take the speck out of your eye,' when all the time there is a plank in your own eye" (Matthew 7:3–4)?

Now, Jesus wasn't talking to people who just happened to have much greater sins than others. In fact, by the social and religious standards of the first century, the people Jesus was talking to were probably considered better than average. So what is Jesus getting at?

Jesus was helping them, and us, get free from our addiction to the Tree of the Knowledge of Good and Evil. And he was doing it by telling them how to revolt against it. He was in essence instructing them to think the opposite of the way the fruit of the forbidden tree inclines them to think.

When we try to ascribe worth to ourselves at the expense of others—when we judge—we always minimize our own sins and faults and maximize the sins and faults of others. As I was doing in the mall, we feed off of the idolatrous illusion that, however imperfect we may be, at least we are not like *that* person.

As a revolt against this, Jesus says we're to regard our own sins —whatever they happen to be—as plank-sins while regarding other people's sins—whatever they happen to be—as speck-sins. In our own eyes, we are to maximize our sins and faults and minimize the sins and faults of others. Whatever faults we think we see in another, we're to regard our sin as worse. With the apostle Paul, we're to see ourselves as "the worst of sinners" (1 Timothy 1:15–16).

UNLEASHING KINGDOM LIFE

When we revolt against judgment and return to getting all our Life from God, it unleashes the Life of the Kingdom within us. Let me return to my mall experience.

Soon after I woke up to the mental gossip going on in my mind, I could almost hear the Lord gently rebuking me. In effect, he said, "I don't recall appointing you to be judge and jury over people, Mr. Boyd. The job I've given to you is to simply agree with me that each and every person you see is worth me dying for. So I want you to reflect that agreement in your thoughts about them."

It was a much-needed rebuke.

The Lord was really just repeating what Paul taught us when he said we are to "take captive every thought to make it obedient to Christ" (2 Corinthians 10:5). Everything we do is to be done in love, and this obviously includes thinking. Every judgmental thought we entertain is like a cork that blocks the flow of Kingdom Life through us.

As a result of this rebuke, I repented of my mental gossip and committed to striving only to entertain thoughts that expressed unsurpassable worth about people. I started thanking God for each person I saw and privately asking God to bless them.

And almost immediately it was like I'd removed a cork on the geyser of God's infinite love. The wellspring of Life that Jesus says abides in us was being unleashed. I began to experience a love and joy that was absolutely incredible. In that moment it seemed I was not only agreeing with God about each person's unsurpassable worth; I was being empowered to actually see and experience their unsurpassable worth. I wasn't simply loving these people out of duty (as good and necessary as that is). I was experiencing love for these people.

It was beautiful. It was the Kingdom.

I knew in that moment that this is what it is to receive and manifest Kingdom Life. This is what it is to love as Christ loved me. This is what it feels like to become free from idols and judgment.

Over the last decade or so I've striven to make blessing people an automatic habit of my thoughts. I still have a long way to go, and I can't claim that I usually experience anything like the depth of love and joy I experienced that day in the mall, though occasionally I do.

But this is as it should be. The purpose of agreeing with God about every person we encounter isn't for us to experience something. If that happens, wonderful. But the purpose is to simply align our hearts and minds with God. The purpose is to be, on a moment-by-moment basis, submitted to God's loving reign. And whether we experience anything or not, in the process of doing this we are manifesting the beauty of the Kingdom revolution and revolting against the ugliness of all judgment.

Viva la revolution!

CHAPTER 5

THE REVOLT
AGAINST RELIGION

Truly I tell you, the tax collectors and the prostitutes
are entering the kingdom of God ahead of you.

JESUS (MATTHEW 21:31)

My relationship prevents me from having a religion.

SLOGAN ON A COOL T-SHIRT I OFTEN WEAR

I SMOKED MY FIRST JOINT WHEN I WAS TWELVE, DROPPED MY FIRST HIT
of acid at thirteen, and spent the next four years doing the late '60s
and early '70s "sex, drugs, and rock and roll" thing. I was searching
for "the lost chord" while taking a few too many "magical mystery
tours" to "the dark side of the moon."

Then, at the age of seventeen, I "got religion."

I mean—I *really* got religion.

I found it in the holiness Pentecostal church my ("backslidden")
girlfriend was raised in. She invited me because she thought I'd find
it amusing. Besides, bringing visitors would help her win a Sunday
school contest. I was desperately searching for something, and the
lively church services and exuberant people kept me coming back
week after week. Before too long, I responded to an alter call and
surrendered my life to Jesus.

Being "saved" in this church meant that you didn't go to movies
and didn't drink alcohol, use tobacco, or do any drugs. Nor were
we supposed to listen to secular music or go to professional sports
events (never quite got that one). The women only wore dresses
(always extending beneath their knees), the men never wore facial

hair, and the women never cut their hair or wore makeup. We thought all people who didn't live according to our holiness standards were going to hell.[1]

This was "religion" with a vengeance.

This wasn't all bad. I think I may have needed this sort of radical break in my life to put an end to some of the destructive behavioral patterns I'd developed over my first seventeen years. Not only this, but I had genuine encounters with Jesus in the midst of all this religion. I did, in fact, get "saved," and I'm forever grateful for my experience in the Pentecostal church.

But I also discovered—very quickly—that I wasn't good at this religion thing. I wasn't good at it as a kid in Catholic school, and I was no better at it when I was seventeen and getting off drugs. As they used to say of backsliders in my church, I "just couldn't live the life."

After several years of failure and self-condemnation, I gave up. If religion was what saved people, I concluded, I was destined for hell.

I was right. Fortunately, I came to realize that religion doesn't save people. Religion, in fact, may be one of the greatest *obstacles* to being saved. To participate in the fullness of Life that comes from God, we must revolt against the idolatrous life offered us from religion.

IDOLATRY AND RELIGION

At this point some readers may be getting upset—or at least confused. Isn't Jesus the founder of Christianity, the one true religion? How can a Christian author suggest that Kingdom people are supposed to revolt against religion?

Please hear me out. It is a crucial, though subtle, point.

When I speak of religion, I'm referring to any system of beliefs and behaviors people embrace and engage in as a means of ascribing transcendent worth to themselves. It's a means for people to experience a worth that they believe goes beyond what anything in this world can give them. As I use the term, therefore, religious people feed the hunger of their heart by striving to impress whatever picture of God or gods they embrace with the rightness of their beliefs and behaviors—in contrast to the wrongness of others' beliefs and behaviors.

While wealth, power, and sex are the most prevalent idols in Western culture today, religion is historically the most common idol people latch onto. It's also proven to be the most dangerous.

Here's why. While all idols instill a particular version of the Tree of the Knowledge of Good and Evil within us, religion often inclines people to give their version of the Tree of the Knowledge of Good and Evil *divine authority*. And while all idols incline people to act aggressively to protect and advance their "good" and resist what they judge to be "evil," religion often gives this "good" and "evil" *eternal significance*. Religion significantly "ups the ante" on idolatry and judgment. So it's not surprising that religion has often inspired violence throughout history and continues to do so today.

For the same reason, religious idolatry is particularly resistant to the Kingdom of God. It's no coincidence that the main opposition Jesus faced in establishing the Kingdom came from the guardians of the religious status quo—the Pharisees, religious scribes, and the like. So it should not surprise us that the main opposition to advancing the Kingdom in our own day comes from contemporary guardians of the religious status quo.

To establish and manifest the beautiful Kingdom in his day, Jesus had to revolt against religion. To advance and manifest the beautiful Kingdom today, we must do the same.

THE KINGDOM AND THE CHRISTIAN RELIGION

But isn't the Christian religion an exception, you might ask? After all, in contrast to all other religions, this religion professes the truth.

I don't dispute that Christianity professes important truths. Nor am I suggesting that faithfulness to the Kingdom requires followers of Jesus to revolt against any particular Christian doctrines (or even reject true things they find in other religions, for that matter).

The Kingdom's revolt against religion, including the Christian religion, is on a totally different level. It is a revolt against all attempts to get Life from particular beliefs—including true ones. For where God truly reigns over an individual or a community, their only source of Life is God, *not* the rightness of their beliefs.

THE ALL-IMPORTANT CRITERION

If you're still puzzled, try thinking about it this way.

In the last chapter we saw that the New Testament teaches that expressing Christlike love is the most important aspect of the Kingdom, compared to which nothing else really matters. In this light, what are we to think of the Christian church when, in the name of Christ and for the glory of God, it engages in violence against its enemies?[2] The Church that tortured and murdered heretics, Muslims, witches, and Jews was certainly orthodox in its core beliefs. Yet—call me crazy if you will—it seems to me this barbaric activity wasn't expressing Christlike love. And since the New Testament teaches that anything that doesn't express Christlike love is devoid of Kingdom value—no matter how true and impressive it might otherwise be—we can only conclude that the Church that engaged in this anti-Christ activity was not the Kingdom.

Jesus never tortured or murdered his enemies. He gave his life for them. Insofar as Christianity motivated people to torture or murder enemies rather than die for them, it wasn't following Jesus. It wasn't part of the Kingdom.

It really is that simple.

WHO'S THE REAL HERETIC?

If love is above every other consideration, and if everything without love is devoid of Kingdom value, as the New Testament teaches, then it seems we should regard the command to love to be the ultimate test of orthodoxy. To fail to love like Jesus is the worst form of heresy, regardless of how true one's beliefs are. Demons believe true things, James tells us, but their true beliefs are worthless because they are not accompanied with works that reflect God's love.

In the sixteenth century John Calvin had Michael Servetus burned at the stake for denying that Jesus was the eternal Son of God and for rejecting infant baptism.[3] Servetus' denial of Jesus' deity was indeed unorthodox, but in light of the all-or-nothing emphasis of the New Testament on manifesting Christlike love, how can we avoid concluding that Calvin was himself guilty of a far worse heresy?

Church history is full of people being tortured and put to death for such heresies as not acknowledging the authority of the Church, baptizing wrongly, and denying the Trinity. Yet we don't have any record of anyone so much as having their hand slapped for embracing the worst heresy imaginable—namely, failing to love and do good to one's enemies, as Jesus commanded. That leaves me speechless!

Defenders of the tradition sometimes argue that we can't hold ancient Christians to modern humanitarian standards. Life in the ancient world was just more violent, they claim.

This argument, however, is not very compelling. Jesus and the early church lived in eras that were at least as violent as any in Church history, yet they managed to love their enemies rather than engage in violence against them. The same could be said of a number of individuals and groups throughout Church history. For example, when Calvinists, Lutherans, and Anglicans tortured and killed Anabaptists in the sixteenth and seventeenth centuries, the victims followed the example of Jesus and refused to fight back. Their faithfulness to the Kingdom bears witness against the faithlessness of those professing Christians who persecuted them.[4]

This is not to suggest that we can pass judgment on Calvin or anyone else in Church history. We are ourselves sinners who have planks sticking out of our eyes, so we must leave all judgment up to the One who alone knows the innermost hearts of people. But this doesn't mean we can't discern what is and is not the Kingdom. We can't place ourselves above others—not even those who murdered "in Jesus' name." But we can and must clearly separate torturing and killing in Jesus' name (or for any other reason) from the beautiful, Christlike Kingdom. Insofar as the Church engaged in activities like this, it was involved in the most heinous form of heresy imaginable—its orthodox beliefs notwithstanding.

Whenever we get our worth, significance, and security from the rightness of our personal or national religion rather than from God, we will inevitably fall into the heresy of failing to love. We can only manifest the beautiful Life of the Kingdom if we receive this beautiful Life from the King.

A DIFFERENT KIND OF HOLINESS

One of the most shocking aspects of Jesus' ministry is that he befriended tax collectors, prostitutes, and other "sinners." He even went to parties with them! They seemed to want to hang out with Jesus. This tells us something important about the Kingdom of God.

Prostitutes and tax collectors were ranked at the bottom of the righteousness scale in first-century Jewish religion. These two groups epitomized everything this religion stood against. Prostitutes were viewed as undermining the moral fabric of society, while tax collectors were seen as traitors because they worked for the oppressive Roman government, which most Jews despised. No wonder Jesus' association with these groups ruined his reputation among religious leaders (see, for example, Matthew 9:11; Mark 2:16; and Luke 5:30).

The contrast between Jesus and the religious leaders of his day gets us to the heart of the difference between the Kingdom and religion. Though Jesus was sinless, prostitutes and tax collectors wanted to hang out with him. His kind of holiness didn't repel sinners. It attracted them. By contrast, prostitutes, tax collectors, and other sinners stayed far away from the Pharisees and other guardians of the religious status quo. The "holiness" of the religious crowd repelled them.

Why this stark difference? Because Jesus and the Pharisees had two radically different ways of being holy.

The word *holy* means "consecrated," or, literally, "set apart." Jesus was set apart by living in perfect submission to God and perfectly manifesting the Life of God. This is the Life everyone hungers for, so prostitutes, tax collectors, and other sinners found themselves drawn to him. Something about the holiness of Jesus made them feel more fully alive than they'd ever felt before.

The "holiness" of the Pharisees and other religious leaders was of a different sort. What "set them apart," in their view, was how they contrasted with people like tax collectors and prostitutes. At its core, their idea of "holiness" was predicated on their religious idolatry.

While the holiness of Jesus ascribed unsurpassable worth to people, the "holiness" of the Pharisees detracted worth from people as they ascribed worth to themselves. The holiness Jesus manifested fed people, while the judgmental "holiness "of the Pharisees fed off of people.

Jesus' holiness manifested the unique and beautiful holiness of the Kingdom, and it contrasts with the ugly, idolatrous "holiness" of religion in the strongest possible way.

THE WARFARE BETWEEN THE KINGDOM AND RELIGION

Religious leaders of Jesus' day knew that if Jesus' way of living and loving reveals what God is truly like, they could no longer feel special and worthwhile before God on the basis of how they contrasted with robbers, evildoers, adulterers, tax collectors, and prostitutes. The same is true today.

If Life can only be received from God for free, then all the other ways religious people try to find God's Life are worthless.

If God's estimation of people is based completely on what he has done for people on Calvary, not on what people do for him, then religious people can no longer get Life from the fact that they are set apart from others because of their right beliefs and behaviors.

If the way Jesus attracted sinners is what it looks like when God reigns, then the way religious people repel sinners must be against God's reign.

If Jesus manifests the Kingdom of God, then, as Jesus explicitly taught, the tax collectors and the prostitutes are entering the kingdom of God ahead of religious idolaters like the Pharisees (Matthew 21:31). Nothing could have been more shocking to a first-century Jewish religious audience than this statement.

The Kingdom revolution cuts to the heart of religion and forces idolaters to make an important decision. They must either repent, which means turning from their religion as a source of Life, or they must cling to their religion as a source of Life and resist, at all costs, the movement Jesus came to establish.

The majority of the religious leaders in Jesus' day chose the latter — which is why they crucified him.

WHERE ARE THE PROSTITUTES?

Let's bring this closer to home by asking: What kind of holiness does the Western Church manifest today? To answer this, we need only ask: Are the prostitutes and tax collectors of our day attracted to us or repelled by us?

While there are wonderful examples of Kingdom communities who attract, embrace, and transform those who are most judged and marginalized by society and religion today, on the whole today's prostitutes and tax collectors steer as far away from Christians as they did the Pharisees in the first century.

Nothing could be a greater indictment of the modern Church than this.

Jesus was known for the scandalous way he loved. The religious people viewed him as an anarchist eroding the moral fabric of society because of his refusal to recognize their all-important distinction between their "holiness" and all they judged to be "unholy."

Tragically, Christians today often see themselves as the primary defenders and promoters of this very distinction. Rather than viewing themselves as "the worst of sinners," as Jesus and Paul command, many view themselves as the morally superior guardians of society who will protect it from those they judge to be "the worst of sinners." So, instead of being known as outrageous lovers, Christians are largely viewed as self-righteous judgers.[5]

No wonder the prostitutes and tax collectors of our day are repelled by us.

It's time for the Church to free itself from the religious holiness of the Pharisees and begin to manifest the holiness of the Kingdom. It's time for us to realize that our calling is to serve people sacrificially —including prostitutes, tax collectors, and enemies—rather than judging them. It's time we cease getting Life from the rightness of our beliefs and behaviors and return to getting it from the one true source of Life.

Viva la revolution!

CHAPTER 6

THE REVOLT
AGAINST INDIVIDUALISM

If we have no peace, it is because we have forgotten
that we belong to each other.

MOTHER TERESA

No man is an island, entire of itself;
every man is a piece of the continent, a part of the main.

JOHN DONNE

FROM QUASI-AUTISTIC LONER
TO COMMUNITY ENTHUSIAST

A friend once described me as "charmingly eccentric." I'm not sure
about "charming," but I can't deny the "eccentric." I'm not eccentric
like Howard Hughes or "Rain Man." Just, perhaps, a wee bit short
of completely normal. In fact, I've had two experts on autism tell
me I have certain "autistic characteristics."

It's weird. While the Myers-Briggs Inventory test lists me as an
introvert, I instinctively act like an extrovert around people. I genuinely love people, and even love being around them—in limited
doses. After any prolonged social interaction, however, I have to
retreat into my "cave" (as my wife, Shelley, calls it).

When Shelley and I were married in 1979 we had two major
issues to work through. First, we had to negotiate how much time
I spent in my cave versus how much time I spent with her. We've
been married twenty-nine years, and we still at times have to negotiate that one. Second, we had to negotiate how much time I spent
in my cave versus how much time we as a couple spent with other
people. It took awhile, but this one we've actually resolved.

You see, like most normal people, Shelley wanted us to make friends with other couples. I was fine with this, theoretically speaking. But when it came to actually doing it, I usually resisted. The books in my cave just seemed more stimulating and less draining than actual people. But one must make sacrifices to keep a marriage working, so Shelley on occasion managed to drag me to these get-togethers.

Then, slowly, a curious thing began to happen. I discovered that every now and then I actually enjoyed visiting people rather than staying in my cave. I even discovered, slowly but surely, that people could sometimes be *more* interesting than books—just in a different way.

Over time, I actually began to feel I *needed* to get together with people. A certain vacancy in my life, which I wasn't even aware of before, seemed to get filled when I was in close relationships with people.

Today, I can't believe how my life has changed.

For the last sixteen years my wife and I have belonged to a small community of people that has become so close that I can't imagine living without them. Our community has evolved over the years, but four couples, including Shelley and myself, have consistently formed its core. We have an extended small group that includes about thirty people, including our kids and some younger friends.

Once a week (on average) our group gets together to pray, worship, minister to people in our neighborhood, go to movies, play games, go out to eat, dance, or just hang out. We usually have a great time. If I may modestly say so, we're so much fun our kids (most of whom are now young adults) often *want* to hang out with us.

Over the years we've laughed, cried, fought, made up, shared hopes and disappointments, and grown together. We've helped raise each other's children, fix each other's homes, work on each other's cars, and mend—and sometimes rescue—each other's marriages. We've helped each other work through personal issues as well as a vast array of relational conflicts and spiritual struggles. We've helped refine each other's politics, construct each other's theologies, and grown in our commitment to radical Kingdom living.

When the husband of one of the couples lost his job, the rest of us pooled our resources to support the family for the four months it took for him to get back to work.

At least once a year we take a weeklong vacation together. Our kids often join us.

The guys in the group are all musicians, so we formed a band that plays '70s and '80s classic rock as well as some contemporary worship music. I'm the drummer. We're called *Not Dead Yet*. We're not great, but we have a lot of fun and raise a lot of money for charities.

One of the couples in our group felt led to start a ministry to impoverished children in Haiti, so we all pooled our resources to help support it. Out of this ministry several other ministries in Haiti have evolved that we're also involved in.[1] At least once a year those who are able travel to Haiti to tend to these ministries, sometimes taking their kids with them. A few of our kids and friends have lived and ministered in Haiti for extended periods of time.

Six years ago, we all began to feel God calling us to move out of the suburbs into the city. We now live on the same city street within a couple blocks of each other. Until a decade and a half ago, I dreamed of living far out in the country, on the top of a mountain, or in an isolated cabin in the middle of a deep forest. I now find myself living in the middle of a densely populated city surrounded by an amazing diversity of people — and I love it!

As a result of our new proximity, our level of interdependence increased even more. We now share everything from cars and shovels to salt, salad dressing, and even showers (we all live in older houses where things don't always work).

Our new location has also opened up new ministry opportunities. For example, we now partner with a nonprofit social-service agency that serves elderly and mentally disabled shut-ins in the inner city. As needs arise, we get together to repair homes, mow lawns, shovel snow, buy groceries, lead Bible studies, or just hang out with these dear people. You get the picture.

This alleged autistic-tending loner has discovered the profound beauty of deeply committed relationships, and I've discovered that *this* is how life is meant to be lived—regardless of how introverted a person might be.

Now, don't get me wrong; I still need a lot of time in my cave. My friends accept this. Half the time while we're on vacation, they are out doing stuff while I hang back, read, write, and just think. I've learned that being in community doesn't threaten my individuality. To the contrary, it enhances it.

Everyone in our group has eccentricities that the others accept and make good-natured fun of. It's these very differences, working together, that make our group interesting and, with work, beautiful.

God created each of us unique. But this uniqueness was meant to be woven into the tapestry of community. We are made in the image of the triune God, whose essence is a loving community. We are created for community. This is how Jesus lived, and it's how his followers are called to live.

THE IDOL OF INDIVIDUALISM

In chapter 1 we noted that the world is oppressed by fallen Powers that influence human culture in ways contrary to God's will. One primary way the Powers operate in modern Western culture is by promoting an ideology of "rugged individualism," which runs directly counter to God's will for us to live in community. We place unprecedented stress on our individual freedoms and rights. While people in traditional cultures tend to define themselves by their ties to a particular community, modern westerners tend to define themselves *apart* from ties to a particular community—"over and against" others instead of "in relation" to others.

This tendency toward individualism has been greatly intensified by the hedonistic consumer culture we've created over the last century. We tend to measure our worth by what we are able to purchase. This in turn conditions us to make striving after things—pursuing "the American dream"—a higher priority than cultivating deep, committed relationships. Meaningful relationships take time, and that is something people indoctrinated into the consumer mindset never feel like they have.

On top of this, the wealth of options our consumer culture offers conditions us to expect to have things our way. This also undermines our desire and capacity for deep, meaningful relationships, for this type of relationship requires that we be willing to sometimes forgo our preferences and put up with things we don't care for.

When you combine our relationship-eroding consumerism with our stress on individual freedoms and rights, you can understand why most westerners have many acquaintances but few (if any) deeply committed relationships that echo the beautiful love of the triune God.

In his marvelous little book *The Great Divorce*, C. S. Lewis envisioned hell as a realm in which people are forever moving farther away from one another. Hell is the ultimate, cosmic, suburban sprawl. It's a vision of hell that is becoming a reality in Western culture, and it's something Kingdom people in the West are called to passionately revolt against.

WHAT NIGERIANS HAVE THAT AMERICANS LACK

In the West we are brainwashed into thinking that clinging to our personal rights and freedoms, while striving after things, is our ticket to happiness. In reality, it's making us miserable.

Several studies have revealed that, statistically speaking, America has one of the highest rates of depression (and other mental health disorders) in the world. On the other hand, these mental health studies suggest that Nigeria has one of the lowest rates of depression.[2] Despite the fact that the average standard of living in America is roughly four times that of Nigeria, and despite the fact that Nigeria is a country with a multitude of social problems—including dehumanizing poverty, a serious AIDS epidemic, and ongoing civil strife—Nigeria has far less depression, per capita, than America.

What do Nigerians have that Americans lack?

Judging from the Nigerians I know, I'm convinced the main thing is a sense of community. Nigerians generally know they need one another. They don't have the luxury of trying to do life solo, even if they had the inclination to do so. Consequently, Nigerians tend to have a sense of belonging that most Americans lack, and this provides them with a sense of general satisfaction in life, despite the hardships they endure.

Many studies have shown that personal happiness is more closely associated with one's depth of relationships and the amount one invests in others than it is with the comforts one "enjoys." And this is exactly what we'd expect given that we're created in the image of a God whose very nature is communal. It's against our nature to be isolated. It makes us miserable, dehumanizes us, and ultimately destroys us.

A "ONE-ANOTHER" COMMUNITY

Jesus revolted against the Powers that fragment relationships by modeling what communal life under the reign of God looks like. Though he was the Son of God, he didn't try to "go solo" in his life and ministry. He had a network of friends, like Mary and Martha, he could rely on when he traveled. He banded with a group of twelve disciples who traveled and ministered with him. And he chose three people (Peter, James, and John) to form his most intimate circle of friends. His life manifested the truth that where God reigns, individuals will be united together in close-knit communities.

The earliest Christians understood this. They met regularly as a large group in the temple courts, hearing and studying "the apostles' teaching" and enjoying fellowship with one another. But they also met in smaller groups inside each other's homes on a daily basis where they shared meals and prayed together.

These earliest disciples shared everything they owned with one another so that no one in their community was in need. In a culture that had no social "safety nets," this was an aspect of the early Church that made it attractive to outsiders.

House gatherings were the primary social unit of the Jesus revolution for the first three centuries. When Paul addresses a letter to "the church" at a certain location, we mustn't think there was a large church building located in that region in which all the Christians congregated. Buildings specially designed to be churches didn't exist until Christianity was legalized and began to attract prestigious and powerful people in the fourth century. When Paul addresses "the church" at a certain location, he's addressing a body of disciples who gathered in various privately owned houses scattered throughout the city. His letter would be read in one house church, then copied and passed on to other house gatherings.

Many of the New Testament's teachings about how Christians are to relate to one another only make sense when we understand them in a small house-church context. For example, the New Testament commands us to submit to one another, confess sins to one another, encourage one another, serve one another, and hold one another accountable. How can we authentically do this unless we're in intimate relationships with one another? These aren't the kinds of things you can do by meeting in a large building once a week with people you hardly know.

THE INVENTION OF McCHURCH

This isn't to say there's anything inherently unbiblical about larger Kingdom gatherings. The book of Acts suggests the earliest Christians met in larger groups when they could. I myself pastor a church that holds weekend services attended by a couple thousand people, and it accomplishes some good things. But by New Testament standards, large group meetings—the typical American church model—are not adequate.

Among other shortcomings, the large-group, weekend-event model of church fails to confront the individualism we're in bondage to. In fact, if we're not careful, the weekend-event model of church can actually pander to our individualism.

Think about it. Once a week we go *to* church (a religious building) rather than seeing ourselves *as* the church. As good consumers we typically choose our church based on our own preferences, conveniences, and needs. Since we're conditioned to assume that "the customer is always right," we believe we have the right to have things our way. If one church fails to please us we simply shop for another that will. Since there are only so many of us religious consumers to go around, churches have to compete with one another to acquire and keep as many consumers as possible. This, of course, puts pressure on pastors to sweeten the religious product they're peddling by adding as many blessings as possible to their messages and by refraining from saying or doing anything that might drive consumers away.

Welcome to McChurch, where you get served up a Gospel tailor-made to suit your personal tastes and needs and that never confronts you or causes you any discomfort.

McChurch not only fails to confront the idols and pagan values of Western culture, it often "Christianizes" them. Not only do we not have to give up our possessions, as Jesus commands; we're told that following Jesus ensures that we'll get *more* of them! Not only do we not have to love and serve our enemies, as Jesus commands; we're told that God is on our side when we applaud our nation bombing them!

If you're looking for an explanation as to why studies confirm there's hardly any difference in Western countries between churchgoers and non-churchgoers in terms of the core values we embrace, I suggest you've just found it.

GROWING TOGETHER IN CHRIST

Against the theology and practices of McChurch, Kingdom people are called to live and minister in community with others. We cannot hope to manifest the Kingdom if we are doing life "solo."

The Bible says we are all members of the body of Christ. A member of our physical body that becomes detached stops growing and becomes useless. So too, we can only grow and reach our full potential in the Kingdom if we remain attached to the body of Christ. The Kingdom suffers, and we suffer, when we try to do life solo.

We all need people we are committed to loving and serving and who are committed to loving and serving us. We all need people who are close enough to us to notice when we're discouraged and who care enough to take time to encourage us. We all need people who can spot areas of weakness in our life and care enough to confront us in love. We all need people who can notice when we're going astray and who care enough to hold on to us. We all need a community that helps us revolt against those dominant aspects of our culture that are inconsistent with the Kingdom life. And all of us—even quasi-autistic loners like me—need a community with whom we can share the joys, sorrows, victories, and defeats of ordinary life. It's essential for our wholeness and Kingdom effectiveness, and it's essential if we are to reflect the communal love of the triune God in our life.

Close-knit, loving, mutually submitted, and mutually accountable relationships—these are the primary context in which God transforms us and uses us to transform the world. If we can think of the Kingdom as a spiritual army (which it *is*), then we'd say the commander has decided that small platoons are the primary place where soldiers are to be equipped for battle and the primary unit he uses to engage in battle.

In the process of belonging to and fighting within a platoon, we learn how to manifest the beauty of the communal Kingdom while revolting against the destructive individualism of our culture and the Powers that fuel it. In community, the beautiful revolution advances.

Viva la revolution!

CHAPTER 7

THE REVOLT
AGAINST NATIONALISM

Our citizenship is in heaven.

PHILIPPIANS 3:20

Nationalism is an infantile disease.
It is the measles of mankind.

ALBERT EINSTEIN.

WASHING OSAMA'S FEET

A friend of mine hired artist Lars Justinen to paint the picture on the previous page to use on posters advertising a conference on the character of God that he was hosting.[1] He had contracts with several malls to hang these advertisements. Almost immediately after hanging the posters, however, the malls began to be flooded with angry calls—mostly from Christians—demanding they be taken down. They were outraged at the image of Jesus washing Osama Bin Laden's feet. So strong was the outcry that the malls decided they had to cancel their contracts and take down the posters. The Christian college that was renting space to my friend rescinded its contract as well.

Apparently, the protesters believe that Jesus would *not* wash Osama Bin Laden's feet. And why would they think this? Presumably, it's because these protesters assume that any enemy of America is an enemy of Jesus and that Jesus would not wash the feet of his (and therefore America's) enemies.

It's a curious belief. If Jesus was willing to suffer a hellish death on behalf of Bin Laden, how can we imagine he'd balk at washing his feet?

This episode reveals the extent to which many American Christians have allowed their faith to be co-opted by nationalism. Many have allowed their allegiance to the flag to compromise their allegiance to the cross. They've allowed the values of the empire they live in to redefine the Jesus they believe in.

Rather than obediently agreeing with God that every person—including Osama Bin Laden—was worth Jesus' dying for, they've reduced Jesus to a pagan tribal deity who, of course, agrees with them. If *they* would rather kill Bin Laden than wash his feet, then surely *Jesus* must want this as well.

The truth is that the real Jesus bears no resemblance to this tribal Jesus. The real Jesus is reflected on the poster!

A NATION TO REUNITE THE NATIONS

To appreciate how important revolting against nationalism is to the Kingdom, we need to review a little Bible history.

God's dream has always been for humans to form a single, united community under his loving Lordship. His goal has always been for humans to reflect the love of the triune God by how we relate to one another. This dream was shattered when our sin set us against one another and divided us into different tribes and nations. But God did not give up on his dream.

He called Abraham to form a unique nation by which "all peoples on earth will be blessed." The unique calling of the descendents of Abraham (the Jews) was to become a nation of servant-priests whom God would use to reunite the nations under his loving Lordship.

This vision of a reunited humanity is hammered home with increasing clarity and strength throughout the Old Testament. For example, Jeremiah looks forward to the time when "all nations will gather in Jerusalem to honor the name of the Lord." Zechariah prophesies of a time when the Lord will "be king over the whole earth" so that he will be the only Lord confessed among the nations. And Joel prophesies of a time when God's Spirit would be poured out "on all people."

But the prophet who most forcefully captures God's vision of a reunited humanity is Isaiah. From the start, the Israelites had a tendency to define themselves over and against other nations rather than as the servants of other nations. They fell into nationalistic idolatry. Through Isaiah the Lord confronts this idolatrous mindset and reiterates his agelong goal of reaching all nations.

In Isaiah 55 the Lord announces that anyone from any nation who is thirsty or hungry can come and feast at his banquet table for free. He promises everyone who comes to his feast that he will bring them into the "everlasting covenant" that he "promised to David." For, the Lord says, David was raised up not just to be the earthly king of the Jews but also to be a "witness" and "ruler" of all nations. It's clear from this that God's goal was, and still is, to incorporate all nations into his covenant with Israel under the reign of a Davidic King.

The Lord reiterates his global goal when he goes on to say that his chosen people will "summon nations you know not, and nations you do not know will come running to you" because the Lord "has endowed you with splendor." God's goal was always to bless Israel as a means of attracting all nations to himself. Most Israelites forgot this, however. They thought the blessing was just because God favored them over other nations. They had reduced Yahweh to a tribal deity.

And so the Lord goes on to proclaim,

> *My thoughts are not your thoughts,*
> *neither are your ways my ways....*
> *As the heavens are higher than the earth,*
> *so are my ways higher than your ways*
> *and my thoughts than your thoughts.*
> Isaiah 55:8–9

People often cite this verse to justify embracing incoherent beliefs. A convenient way to insulate a cherished belief from rational criticism is to simply say, "God's thoughts are higher than our thoughts." It's really an abusive use of this passage, for in the original context God is confronting our tribalism. God is saying his thoughts are higher than ours, for like the ancient Jews, we often forget that God's heart is for all people from all nations to come and feast at his banquet table for free.

One final aspect of the Old Testament's unfolding vision of a reunited humanity should be mentioned. Throughout the Old Testament we find a growing expectation that someday all the nations will be reunited under a divinely appointed king.

In Psalm 72, for example, the author prays for a day when "all kings" and "all nations" will "bow down" to a king whom God will anoint. God's king will deliver "the needy who cry out" and save "the afflicted who have no one to help." He will "take pity on the weak and the needy and save the needy from death." He will "rescue them from oppression and violence, for precious is their blood in his sight." When this happens, the psalmist concludes, "all nations will be blessed through [God's anointed king]" and "the whole earth" will "be filled with his glory."

What passages like this reveal is that God's promise to bless all the nations through Abraham and his descendents is to be fulfilled in a coming king whom God will anoint. Through him all the scattered people groups will be ministered to. Through him all the tribes and nations will be reconciled as they come to know the one true God. Through him God's dream of a united human community reflecting his triune love will be finally realized.

THE TRANSNATIONAL KINGDOM OF JESUS

The anointed king, of course, is Jesus Christ. (*Christ* means "anointed.")

When the New Testament announces that Jesus Christ is Lord of all, as it frequently does, it has to be understood against the backdrop of this Old Testament motif. Jesus Christ is not just the Lord, Savior, and Messiah of the Jews: he is the Lord, Savior, and

Messiah of all people. In him, all the prophecies about the nations being reunited will eventually find their fulfillment.

The theme is unmistakable if we read the Gospels against the backdrop of their original social and political milieu. Most Jews of Jesus' day were intensely nationalistic and were expecting a completely pro-Israel Messiah. They thought the Messiah would lead Israel to victory over their Roman oppressors and would reestablish Israel as a sovereign nation under God.

This is why people constantly tried to force Jesus' hand on the divisive political issues of the day. But as we noted in Chapter 2, Jesus uniformly refused to weigh in on these debates. He would not play the role of a pro-Israel, anti-Roman Messiah or let himself be co-opted by any nationalistic agenda—not even on behalf of God's "chosen nation." For the Kingdom that Jesus came to establish is about fulfilling God's dream of reuniting all the nations.

Jesus reveals that, where God reigns, national walls will be torn down and national distinctions rendered insignificant. "In Christ," Paul says, "there is neither Jew nor Gentile." In Christ "the dividing wall of hostility" has been abolished between groups of people and a "new humanity" has been created. A central aspect of the Kingdom revolution, therefore, is manifesting the beauty of what it looks like for a people to be freed from the idol of nationalism and to be reunited under the God who is Lord of all nations.

CHRIST BECOMES A WARRING, TRIBAL GOD

For the first three hundred years or so of the Kingdom revolution, Christians on the whole remained beautifully free of nationalistic idolatry. The early Christians didn't see themselves as belonging to the empire they lived in, and they would not pledge allegiance to or fight for any ruler or country. They routinely choose to die rather than pledge allegiance to a symbolic statue of the emperor. They were consequently criticized and persecuted for being unpatriotic, subversive, and cowardly.

By their refusal to conform and willingness to suffer, these early followers of Jesus bore witness to a radically different, beautiful, Christlike way of doing life. (The word *martyr* originally meant "witness," but it soon became synonymous with witnessing by dying.) In sharp contrast to Islam, which experienced explosive growth in its earliest years by the ferocity of its warriors, the early Church experienced explosive growth in its earliest years by the beautiful way followers of Jesus chose to die rather than fight.

Constantine's alleged vision, telling him to go to war under the banner of Christ (discussed in chapter 2), changed all this. Christ was reduced to a pagan, nationalistic god of war. Once Christianity became part of the empire's nationalism, masses converted to it. While many followers of Jesus resisted this watering down of the faith, the Church, on the whole, embraced it. In the minds of thinkers like Eusebius and Augustine, God had blessed the Church by making it a powerful, politically influential institution.

Not surprisingly, in the centuries that followed, the Church, more often than not, lacked the capacity to distinguish clearly between the Kingdom of God and whatever national kingdom it happened to find itself in. Leaders as well as the masses too often embraced their nation's values and goals as though they were God's own. Consequently, the Church was often been reduced to little more than a religious puppet of the government and assigned the job of blessing its nation's causes and military exploits, just as pagan religions have done throughout history.

The Church blessed European kings and armies as they attempted to reclaim the Holy Land, fought infidels, and carried out other "holy" causes throughout the Middle Ages. As the so-called Holy Roman Empire started becoming fragmented along national lines in the late Middle Ages, this nationalistic idolatry resulted in a myriad of intra-Christian nationalistic wars. Divided by national and denominational lines, Christians brutally slaughtered each other—all under the banner of Christ and always "for God and country." There was, for example, the Hundred Years War in the fourteenth and fifteenth centuries, the Eighty Years War in the sixteenth and seventeenth centuries, and the Thirty Years War in the seventeenth century. The wars were so costly and vanquished so much of Europe's population that secular authorities finally had to step in and call a truce (the famous "Peace of Westphalia").

These bloody intra-Christian wars arguably did more to push the West in a secular direction than any other single factor, including the scientific revolution and the Enlightenment. And this simply illustrates the diabolical consequences that follow when Jesus' followers fail to resist the demonic pull toward nationalism.

MANIFEST DESTINY?

Sadly, this nationalistic, militaristic brand of Christianity played a big role in the conquering of America. As all nations have done throughout history, the Europeans who conquered America did it under the banner of a tribal god. It's just that this tribal god wasn't Zeus, Apollo, or Allah: it was Jesus. In the name of the crucified messiah, and "for God and country," white Europeans claimed this land, slaughtered millions of Native Americans, enslaved millions of Africans, and eventually came to rule.

Not only this, but following the tradition of Eusebius and Augustine (as well as pagans throughout history), the success Europeans enjoyed in vanquishing their enemies was viewed as proof that God was on their side. It was "Manifest Destiny," many claimed, that white Europeans were to lord over the land and over non-Europeans.

This idolatrous nationalism has persisted throughout our history. Americans have always been inclined to see their nation as a "Christian" nation, uniquely "under God," uniquely righteous, and uniquely destined by God to transform the world. Many, including a former president, have spoken of America as the "light of the world" and a "holy city set on a hill." Many continue to believe that American soldiers fight "for God and country," for, they assume, we are a just and righteous nation while our enemies are "evildoers."

There is, of course, absolutely no evidence God agrees with any of this—unless, of course, you buy the old pagan argument that military victory is itself proof of divine favor. The myth of America's favored status is simply something we've told ourselves for centuries to buttress national self-identity and motivate our soldiers in war. The myth, in other words, is just our particular version of nationalistic idolatry.

It's time, I believe, for the Church in America to finally free itself completely from this diabolic bondage.

LIFE, LIBERTY, AND THE PURSUIT OF HAPPINESS

When followers of Jesus aren't careful to clearly distinguish the Kingdom from their own nation, we easily end up Christianizing aspects of our national culture we ought to be revolting against.

For example, America is founded on the conviction that everybody has an "inalienable right" to "life, liberty and the pursuit of happiness." Now, politically speaking, I think these rights are the greatest privileges a government could ever give its people. Politically speaking, I'm a fan of the Declaration of Independence. But as a Kingdom person, I have to be careful not to think these values are *Kingdom* values. Indeed, as a follower of Jesus I have to critically assess these values as things I may have to *revolt against* to manifest the unique beauty of the Kingdom. Let's briefly consider each of these rights.

The Right to Life

Americans believe we have the right to defend our lives and our rights when they're threatened, using any means necessary.

This is a noble political right. I personally wouldn't want to live under a government that didn't grant this right to its citizens. Yet as followers of Jesus we must never let political values—even noble ones—define the unique Kingdom that alone has our allegiance.

As Kingdom people we're called to follow the One who surrendered his right to life in order to express God's love for his enemies. We're thus called to manifest the beauty of a life that no longer clings to its right to remain alive and no longer fears death, even at the hands of our enemies. Following Jesus, we're called to manifest the beauty of an outrageously impractical life that would sooner be killed than kill.

So, while we can affirm the right to life as a noble political value, as Kingdom people we have to revolt against the temptation to put this noble value above the value of self-sacrificial love in order to manifest the beauty of the Jesus-looking Kingdom.

The Right to Liberty

We Americans believe we have the right to exercise our free will however we see fit so long as no one gets hurt. And we believe we have the right to have a say in who governs us and how they govern us.

These are noble political rights. I personally wouldn't want to live under a government that didn't grant these rights to its citizens. Yet as Kingdom people we must notice that this value, while politically noble, has brought about massive decadence in our culture. The emphasis on personal freedom has produced a society that is largely characterized by greed, gluttony, self-centeredness, and sexual immorality. This has to curb our enthusiasm for the ideal of freedom somewhat.

Sadly, many American Christians assume personal freedom is an ultimate value that is therefore worth killing and dying for. Indeed, for many, this is the "light" America shines to the world and the reason why we are a "holy city set on a hill." For many, their faith in freedom and their faith in Christ are essentially inseparable. Standing up for freedom at all costs is part of what it means to be a "true Christian."

But one reads nothing about political freedom in the Old or New Testaments. Most importantly, Jesus doesn't say a word about political freedom. The early Church grew and thrived for several hundred years in a context entirely devoid of political freedom; yet never once in their writings do we hear early Christian writers wishing for it or expecting it—let alone fighting for it! Nor does one find any talk about political freedom throughout the rest of Church history before the modern period (the seventeenth and eighteenth centuries). In fact, the Church on the whole strongly *opposed* the concept of people governing themselves when it first began to be discussed in the late Renaissance and Enlightenment periods. How ironic that several hundred years later the majority of western Christians assume political freedom is synonymous with the Christian faith and—even more ironic—worth killing for! This simply demonstrates how thoroughly the faith of many western Christians has been co-opted and redefined by nationalistic ideals.

Personal and political liberty certainly is a noble cultural ideal, but it certainly *is not* a distinctly Kingdom ideal. In fact, on some level, personal liberty is something Kingdom people are called to *revolt against.*

As Kingdom people we're called to imitate the One who never exercised his free will outside the will of his Father. We're called to surrender our freedom and submit our will to God's will, both as he's revealed it in Scripture and as he directs us by his Spirit moment-by-moment. Not only this, but we're called to live in communities in which we surrender our rights and humbly defer to one another.

Our fallen tendency to exercise our free will however we want is something we must revolt against. As we faithfully do this, we manifest something that goes far beyond a noble political value. We manifest the beauty of a life that is no longer addicted to its freedom and rights, for it has found something far better and far more beautiful—the eternal Life that comes from God lived in a community characterized by servant-love.

The Pursuit of Happiness

We Americans believe we have the right to do whatever we need to do to try to find happiness.

Again, this is a noble political ideal. I wouldn't prefer to live under a government that didn't grant us this right. Yet as Kingdom people we must notice the massive negative effect this cultural value has had on people, both inside and outside the Church. Precisely because we give such emphasis to our right to pursue our own happiness, the highest authority for most Americans is their own personal preferences. Almost every decision is made solely on the basis of whether we think it will make us happy and whether we can afford it. And this simply means that, for most Americans, the pursuit of happiness—or, in starker terms, "hedonism"—is the ultimate lord of their lives.

As Kingdom people this is obviously something we must passionately revolt against. We are called to seek God's will above our own happiness. For Kingdom people, it's not enough to ask, "Is this what I want?" and "Can I afford it?" If God indeed reigns over our life, we must allow him to reign over *all* the major decisions we make. Our most fundamental question, then, is not "Is this what *I* want?" but "Is this what *God* wants?" This is what it means to seek first the Kingdom of God, as Jesus commanded.

As we do this, we manifest something far more beautiful than the pursuit of earthly happiness; we manifest Kingdom joy. In Christ we can be free from the addiction to trying to find happiness. In Christ, we have access to the beautiful Life of God that is characterized by fullness of joy, even when our circumstances are unhappy.

OUR SOLE ALLEGIANCE

A number of years ago I attended a basketball game at a Christian school. Just before the game everyone was asked to stand and say the Pledge of Allegiance. So I stood, placed my hand over my heart, and began to recite our national creed. Halfway through, however, I began to wonder what I was doing. I'm called to live as a foreigner in a strange land. I'm called to be a citizen of a Kingdom that is not of this world. I'm called to live as a soldier stationed in enemy occupied territory whose job it is to carry out of the will of my enlisting officer. Yet here I was pledging allegiance not to Christ, but to the flag of this foreign land in which I happened to be stationed.

Early Christians were willing to be martyred rather than express allegiance to the Roman Empire, but here I was expressing allegiance to the American empire. This didn't seem right. I stopped and haven't said the Pledge since. I love America, but I cannot serve two masters. My allegiance must be pledged to Christ alone.

I acknowledge that people have differing opinions about this matter. Some have told me they recite the Pledge to express support for the good things America stands for, not to express their ultimate allegiance to it. Others have told me they do it out of respect for those who have sacrificed their lives to defend our rights and freedoms, but again, not to pledge their ultimate allegiance. Others have told me they do it simply because they feel like a communist if they don't. Fine. My concern isn't with this particular American ritual.

What concerns me is that it doesn't even occur to many American Christians that there *might* be a conflict between their allegiance to Christ and their Pledge of Allegiance to America. Their faith has become so nationalized that they assume these dual allegiances are compatible. This is an idolatrous assumption, and it helps explain why the lives of most American Christians are indistinguishable from the lives of their pagan American neighbors. We're failing to revolt against the pagan values of our nation because the nation, with its pagan values, has our allegiance—to the point that many followers of Jesus don't even recognize the pagan values *as pagan*. They rather think the nation, with its values, is basically "Christian"!

We've been seduced by the Powers.

It's time for Kingdom people in America to be done with this. Our ultimate allegiance cannot be to America or any other country. It cannot be to a flag, democracy, the right to defend ourselves, the right to do what we want, the right to vote, or the right to pursue happiness however we see fit. We are Kingdom people only to the extent that God alone is King of our lives, and thus only to the extent that we revolt against the temptation to make any cultural values or ideas supreme.

THE LIFE THAT HEALS THE NATIONS

In his marvelous vision of the New Jerusalem—a symbol for the fully established Kingdom of God at the end of the age—John says he saw:

a great multitude that no one could count, from every nation, tribe, people and language, standing before the throne and in front of the Lamb. They were wearing white robes and were holding palm branches in their hands. And they cried out in a loud voice:

> *"Salvation belongs to our God,*
> *who sits on the throne,*
> *and to the Lamb"*
>
> Revelation 7:9–10

What a magnificent vision! John sees that when the Kingdom is fully manifested, Satan will be defeated and Christ will reign as "King of the nations." Then people from all the scattered tribes and divided nations will be brought back together to worship him. The kingdom of the world will then become "the Kingdom of our Lord and of his Messiah."

When all people are reconnected with the one true source of Life, they'll no longer need to feast on their tribal version of the forbidden tree, and so the nations will be healed. The unique "glory" of each nation will contribute to the global display of the multifaceted glory of God.

The full manifestation of this beautiful, transnational Kingdom lies in the future. But the job of Kingdom people is to put this beauty on display *now*. If all nations will be reconciled when the Kingdom comes, we're to manifest national reconciliation now. Since the distinctions among nations, governments, and militaries mean "nothing" to God (Isaiah 40:15, 17), they are to mean nothing to us who live under his reign.

As we individually and collectively do this, we manifest the beauty of a Life that has a freedom no government can grant or take away. We manifest the beauty of God's universal love and revolt against the ugly idol of nationalism.

Viva la revolution!

CHAPTER 8

THE REVOLT
AGAINST VIOLENCE

Peace is not merely a distant goal that we seek,
but a means by which we arrive at that goal.

MARTIN LUTHER KING JR.

Can anything be stupider than that a man has the right to kill me
because he lives on the other side of a river and his ruler has a quarrel with mine,
though I have not quarreled with him?

BLAISE PASCAL

On the battlefields of Ypres, Belgium, during the winter of 1914, British and French troops had for weeks been engaged in a fierce battle with the Germans.[1] The two sides were lined up for miles in trenches a mere sixty to eighty yards apart. Both sides had already suffered heavy casualties.

On Christmas Eve, several German troops put small candle-lit Christmas trees outside their trenches and began singing carols. Then, remarkably, some British and French troops began to sing along in their own language. Before long, up and down the miles of opposing lines the enemy soldiers were singing carols together. The miracle of the moment, contrasting so sharply with the hateful killing that had gone on just hours before, brought tears to some men's eyes.

But the real miracle happened next. At some point, soldiers on both sides began raising signs in the enemy's native language wishing them a Merry Christmas and, in some cases, calling for a Christmas reprieve from fighting. After a while, soldiers on both sides slowly began to put down their weapons and venture out of their cold, muddy trenches to greet one another in "No Man's Land," the space between the two sides. Combatants shook hands and began exchanging gifts—tobacco, cognac, newspapers, chocolate, and whatever else they had. There are even reports of enemy soldiers trading spare guns for soccer balls and other items.

With such an informal truce in place, soldiers first buried the decomposing corpses of their fallen comrades. There are several accounts of combatants helping each other bury their dead and holding joint Christian burial services. Then, for the next week, the two sides enjoyed the Christmas season together. Soldiers played soccer. They shared family photos. Where the language barrier could be overcome, friendships were formed (many Germans had gone to school or worked in Britain before the war). There are accounts of certain combatants laughing hysterically (possibly inebriated) as they lay on the ground together at night and used their pistols to shoot at stars rather than at each other.

Unfortunately, when word of the truce got back to the generals on both sides, they were furious. Orders were issued to resume fighting immediately. On January 1, 1915, the killing picked up where it had left off a week earlier. It wouldn't end until another eight million lives had been wasted.

I've sometimes wondered what it must have been like for these soldiers to resume fighting. The night before the young man in the trench across from you was a friend with whom you laughed and shared stories. Now you have to try to kill him. Why? Because he had been born in a different country—something neither of you had any control over.

All countries try to justify their wars with noble sounding slogans: our soldiers fight for God and country, the motherland, honor, justice, truth, equality, freedom, and so on. But these slogans don't alleviate the arbitrariness of who we befriend and who we slaughter. Soldiers almost always fight for the slogan they were indoctrinated to believe and for the country they happened to be born in.

If these soldiers were like the vast majority of tribal warriors throughout history, they believed what they were told by their superiors and assumed it was their sacred, patriotic duty to kill whomever they were told to kill. This mindless obedience is why human history is largely a history of carnage. And it's not as if humanity is outgrowing this trend. It's estimated that 86 *million* people lost their lives in wars between 1900 and 1989. This is more than the combined fatalities of all previous wars of history.

This is madness. Tragically, it's a madness we've grown accustomed to. It seems normal to us. Yet the madness of this "normal" is exposed when our enemies become friends—as happened on that magical Christmas Eve of 1914. As the soldiers bonded, they couldn't help but realize that, had they been born in the same country, they might have become best friends instead of mortal enemies.

Realizing the arbitrariness of such national violence makes it harder to participate in it. Which, of course, is precisely why the generals were outraged by the truce. It's why the British military leaders commanded that artillery fire be *increased* on each subsequent Christmas Eve during the war and why leaders on both sides created policies that called for the regular relocation of soldiers when they were involved in prolonged fighting in close proximity with an enemy.

They had to ensure that friendships could not be forged. They could not afford to have the arbitrariness and madness of war exposed.

You simply can't sustain an effective war unless soldiers remain confident that something more than chance decided who they should kill. To be willing to kill, soldiers must believe they are the good guys who are righteously fighting the bad guys—to defend God, country, truth, justice, equality, freedom, or whatever.

The soldiers of World War I commemorated the Savior's birth by rising above the madness, laying down their arms, and befriending enemies. In this chapter we'll see that followers of Jesus are to commemorate our Savior's birth by living just like that every day of our lives.

A DIFFERENT KIND OF POWER

Jesus was praying in the garden of Gethsemane, when, suddenly, a group of temple guards showed up to arrest him. Peter immediately drew his sword and started swinging it, cutting off a guard's ear.

From the world's point of view, this violence was justified. Peter was simply defending himself and his master. Yet Jesus rebuked him, reminding him that "all who draw the sword will die by the sword." Jesus then pointed out to Peter that if he was interested in force, Jesus himself could have called on more than twelve legions of warring angels. But this, clearly, was not the kind of power Jesus was interested in employing.

Jesus then proceeded to demonstrate the kind of power he *was* interested in—by revealing God's love for his aggressor and healing the man's severed ear. Through his actions, Jesus showed that the Kingdom of God relies not on the power of the sword, but the power of love that seeks to serve and heal enemies. It's the same power he demonstrated several hours earlier when he washed the feet of his disciples, one of whom he knew would betray him, Judas, and one of whom he knew would deny him, Peter.

After this, Jesus was questioned by Pilate, who asked him if he was the king of the Jews. Jesus responded, "My kingdom is not of this world." And then he pointed to his followers' refusal to fight as proof that his Kingdom "is from another place" (John 18:36). While all the kingdoms of the world use violence to fight enemies who threaten them, Jesus commands his followers to refuse violence and serve enemies—regardless of how justified the use of violence might seem by "normal" standards.

After his encounter with Pilate, Jesus was tortured, mocked, and crucified. He had the power to avoid all this, but he chose not to use it. Why? Because he knew that using violence to protect himself, while justified by worldly standards, would not have benefited his enemies, nor would it have manifested God's universal and unconditional love. It would not have manifested what it looks like when God reigns in someone's life.

Had Jesus defeated his foes by asking his followers to fight for him or by calling on legions of angels, he would have manifested a high-powered version of the kingdom of the world, but he would not have manifested the Kingdom of God. Had Jesus conquered his foes by force, he would have locked them into their rebellious stance against him and his Father instead of offering them the possibility of reconciliation. Had Jesus engaged in a "just war" against his foes, he would have legitimized violence rather than defeating it.

By voluntarily giving his life for his enemies—which includes you and me—Jesus made it possible for us to be transformed by the beauty of his love and to be reconciled to God. And the clearest evidence that we are being transformed by God's love and participating in the Kingdom that is not "of this world" is that we adopt the same nonviolent, self-sacrificial stance toward enemies that Jesus had.

PURGING VIOLENCE FROM OUR MINDS

When most people think of violence, they think of physical violence. But the truth is that our actions are only violent because our hearts and minds are violent first.

For this reason, Jesus emphasizes purging violence from our minds as much as from our physical behavior. In Matthew 5:21–26, he reminds people of the Old Testament command not to murder, for "anyone who murders will be subject to judgment" (v. 21). But he goes on to stress that hostile thoughts and emotions against others are as inconsistent with God's reign as actual murder: "I tell you that anyone who is angry with a brother or sister will be subject to judgment" (v. 22).

Violent attitudes are also reflected in violent speech, which is also inappropriate for followers of Jesus. So Jesus adds, "Anyone who says to a brother or sister, '*Raca*,' is answerable to the Sanhedrin.[2] And anyone who says, 'You fool!' will be in danger of the fire of hell" (v. 22, and Matthew 12:36).

Jesus is saying that anyone who harbors anger toward another or makes a slanderous comment stands under the judgment of God as much as if they had actually committed murder. For such thoughts, emotions, and words violate the intrinsic unsurpassable worth of people and are inconsistent with the reign of God.

If we are going to live in the peace-loving way of Jesus, the place for us to start is by "taking every thought captive to Christ" and purging all violence from our minds.

TURNING THE OTHER CHEEK

But Jesus had a good deal to say about purging violence from our behavior as well. He said, "You have heard that it was said, 'Eye for eye, and tooth for tooth.' But I tell you, do not resist an evil person. If anyone slaps you on the right cheek, turn to them the other cheek also" (Matthew 5:38–39).

The Old Testament taught that retaliation against an offending party is justified as long as the retaliation is proportional to the offense. If someone pokes your eye out, for example, you have the right to take out one (but not both) of theirs. This *quid pro quo* mindset is foundational to the ethics of the Old Testament, as evidenced by how much the Old Testament concerns itself with precise reparations to be paid to people who have been wronged in various ways. Amazingly, in the passage we are discussing Jesus announced that this *quid pro quo* has been abolished in the Kingdom he brings.

In sharp contrast to the Old Testament, Jesus teaches that his followers should not "resist an evil person." He then illustrates what he means by telling his disciples to "turn to them the other cheek also" when struck.

Although it might appear that Jesus is telling his followers to be passive, masochistic doormats in the face of evil, that is not what he's suggesting. The word translated "resist" (*antistenai*) doesn't necessarily suggest passivity. Rather, it connotes responding to a violent action with a similar violent action. We aren't to passively let evil have its way, but neither are we to sink to the level of the evil being perpetrated against us by responding in kind. Our response is rather to be consistent with loving the offender.

This sheds light on why Jesus said, "If anyone strikes you on the right cheek, turn to them the other cheek also." He was most likely referring to the practice of Roman guards using the back of their right hand to slap the right cheek of Jewish subjects. This was an insulting slap, used to demean subjects and keep them in their place. Responding to such a strike by offering the left cheek was a way of defiantly rising above the intended humiliation.[3]

The thrust of Jesus' teaching in this passage, then, is that Kingdom people are to respond to evil in a way that doesn't allow the evil they're confronting to define them. We aren't to be passive, and we aren't to be doormats. But because we aren't to be defined by the evil we confront, neither are we to become violent. As we noted above, the *quid pro quo* mindset has been entirely abolished in the Kingdom Jesus brings.

Paul makes the same point: "Do not be overcome by evil, but overcome evil with good" (Romans 12:21). When we respond to hostility by becoming hostile, we allow the evil in the heart of the enemy to define us. We are "overcome by evil." But when we resist the urge to retaliate and instead respond to an enemy with love — feeding them if they're hungry and giving them something to drink if they're thirsty (v. 20) — we allow love to define us and open up the possibility that the enemy will be transformed into a friend. We are overcoming evil with good.

Though refusing to respond to enemies with force may look weak to the "normal" way of thinking, the truth is that the love that refuses to retaliate is the most powerful force in the universe. Laws may control behavior and violence may annihilate enemies, but only this kind of love has the power to transform the heart of an enemy. It's the only response to evil that doesn't perpetuate evil.

LOVING AND SERVING ENEMIES

Not only are Kingdom people forbidden to respond in kind to their aggressors, we're commanded to love and serve them. In contrast to the "holy war" tradition of the Old Testament, in which Israelites were at times commanded to kill enemies, Jesus taught, "Love your enemies, do good to those who hate you, bless those who curse you, pray for those who mistreat you" (Luke 6:27–28).[4]

Note that loving our enemies, according to Jesus, entails doing them good. It is important that we understand this because there's a long and sad Church tradition, dating back to Augustine, that divorces one's loving disposition toward an enemy from one's actions. This allowed Christians to torture and kill their enemies while claiming to love them.

In reality, Jesus doesn't leave open this possibility. Just as God demonstrates his love toward us by acting in self-sacrificial ways to bless us, so we are to demonstrate our love toward even our enemies by acting in self-sacrificial ways toward them—to "bless them." By "love your enemies," Jesus means we must do good to them.

For the first three centuries of Church history Christians followed the example of Jesus and refused to respond to their enemies with violence. Sadly, this was the first thing to go when the Church acquired political power in the fourth century. Because many leaders viewed this political power as a blessing from God rather than a temptation from the enemy (see Luke 4:5–7), Jesus' example of voluntary suffering on behalf of his enemies had to be radically rethought.

Augustine speculated that Jesus' decision to suffer unjustly rather than use coercive force was not intended to be a permanent example for all Christians to follow. Rather, he reasoned, Jesus had to suffer and die unjustly because he was the Savior, and his suffering and death were necessary for us to be freed from the devil and reconciled to God. Now that this has been accomplished, thought Augustine, and now that God (allegedly) had given Christians the power of the sword, it was not only permissible for Christians to use violence when the cause was "just," they had a responsibility before God to do so.

This was the beginning of what's called the "just war" tradition within Christendom.

Whatever one thinks of the just war theory as applied to secular governments, it has no place in the life of Jesus' followers. For, contrary to Augustine, the New Testament is as clear as it can be that Kingdom people are called to follow Jesus' example of suffering unjustly rather than resorting to violence.

Paul commands us to "follow God's example " and to "walk in the way of love, just as Christ loved us and gave himself up for us"—while we were yet enemies of God. Peter encourages us to be willing to suffer injustice out of "reverent fear of God," for "it is commendable if you bear up under the pain of unjust suffering because you are conscious of God." And our model in this is Jesus himself. When people "hurled their insults at him," Peter continues, "he did not retaliate; when he suffered, he made no threats." Instead, Peter says, "He entrusted himself to him who judges justly."

Peter further encourages people facing persecution to "revere Christ as Lord" in "their hearts" by responding to their persecutors with "gentleness and respect." Following the example of Christ who "suffered once for sins, the righteous for the unrighteous, to bring [them] to God," followers of Jesus are to maintain a gentle, loving attitude so that "those who speak maliciously against [their] good behavior in Christ may be ashamed of their slander." Our willingness to suffer serves our enemies, for, as we saw above, it opens the door that they will be convicted and change their ways.

Surely, some would argue, the use of violence must be justified when people are being persecuted for doing good. Yet this is precisely what followers of Jesus are forbidden to do. Instead—contrary to Augustine—we are called to follow the example of Jesus.

THE DISTINCTIVE MARK OF THE KINGDOM

Jesus' teaching to love our enemies was understandably shocking to his original audience—just as it is to us today. Jesus expected as much, which is why, after telling his audience to love their enemies he added that if we only love those who love us and do good to those who do good to us, we're doing nothing more than what everyone naturally does (Luke 6:32–33). But his followers are to be set apart by the radically different way they love. The distinct mark of the reign of God is that God's people love and do good to people who *don't* love them and *don't* treat them well—indeed, to people who hate them, mistreat them, and even threaten to kill them and their loved ones.

To drive home the importance of this, Jesus says that if we love even our enemies, "then your reward will be great, and you will be children of the Most High, because he is kind to the ungrateful and wicked." The parallel in Matthew has Jesus saying, "Love your enemies and pray for those who persecute you that you may be children of your Father in heaven. He causes his sun to rise on the evil and the good, and sends rain on the righteous and the unrighteous."

Just as God is indiscriminately kind to the ungrateful and the wicked, and just as the Father causes the sun to shine and the rain to fall indiscriminately on the evil and the good, so followers of Jesus are to be distinguished by our ability to love indiscriminately. It makes no difference whether the person is a friend or a foe. And this, Jesus emphasizes, is the condition for our receiving a Kingdom reward and for our becoming "children of your Father in Heaven." Our willingness to go against our fallen nature and love and serve enemies rather than resort to violence against them is the telltale sign that we are participants in the Kingdom of God.

NO EXCEPTIONS!

Notice this: there are *no* exception clauses found anywhere in the New Testament's teaching about loving and doing good to enemies. Indeed, Jesus' emphasis on the indiscriminate nature of the love rules out any possible exceptions. The sun doesn't decide on whom it will and will not shine. The rain doesn't decide on whom it will and will not fall. So too, Kingdom people are forbidden to decide who will and will not receive the love and good deeds we're commanded to give.

It's also important to notice that both Jesus and Paul were speaking to people who lived under an often unjust and oppressive

Roman rule. Such oppressors were among the "enemies" Jesus commanded his followers to love. Some of his followers would, before long, actually watch their children and spouses being put to death before being executed themselves. The "enemies" Jesus and Paul were talking about, therefore, included unjust, nationalistic, life-threatening enemies. Followers of Jesus are to love and seek to do good to even these sorts of enemies.

FAITHFULNESS AND EFFECTIVENESS

This teaching strikes many as ludicrous, impractical, unpatriotic, irresponsible, and possibly even immoral. "Surely Jesus expects us to take up arms against Muslim extremists to protect our country and families!" If I had a dollar for every time I've heard something like that response, I'd be a fairly wealthy man.

The objection that the teaching on nonviolence is ludicrous, if not immoral, is nothing new. The nonviolent stance of the earliest Christians invited many of these same objections, as it has whenever Christians throughout history have embraced it.

The New Testament's teaching on nonviolence strikes many of us this way because we are so conditioned by our violent culture that we have trouble imagining any other response to a life-threatening enemy. We are blinded by the pervasive, long-standing assumption that violence is both "normal" and "necessary" to promote good and minimize evil.

In reality, the belief that violence is "normal" and "necessary" is a self-fulfilling prophecy. It confirms itself by bringing about the very violence it expects and deems necessary. If the practice of refusing violence and loving enemies was consistently put into practice, we'd learn that, over the long haul (and with great sacrifice), the nonviolent way of Jesus is far more effective in combating evil than the way of violence. For while the way of violence may appear to curb evil in the short run, it always—*always*—produces more violence in the long run. It's self-perpetuating.

But all of this is really beside the point, for Kingdom people are called to walk in obedience to the example and teachings of Jesus even when it seems to make no sense to do so.

We're called to be faithful to Jesus, not effective at protecting our lives or ridding the world of evil.

To the world's "normal" way of thinking, Jesus' radical posture is indeed ludicrous, impractical, unpatriotic, irresponsible, and even immoral. And it may, in the short run, look like our refusal to participate in the merry-go-round of violence allows evil to win.

We need to remember that this is exactly how matters looked on Good Friday, when the omnipotent God suffered at the hands of evil rather than use coercive force to extinguish it. But under the reign of the sovereign God, Good Friday never has the last word.

Easter is coming.

Our call is to trust that the foolishness of self-sacrificial love will overcome evil in the end. Our call is to manifest the beauty of a Savior who loves indiscriminately while revolting against all hatred and violence. This is the humble mustard seed revolution that will in the end transform the world.

Viva la revolution!

CHAPTER 9

THE REVOLT
AGAINST SOCIAL OPPRESSION

Our loyalties must transcend our race, our tribe, our class,
and our nation; and this means we must develop a world perspective.

MARTIN LUTHER KING JR.

TALKING TO A QUEEN

Several years ago, I had just ended the closing prayer for our church services when a middle-aged woman approached me. She was wearing a tattered, stained, dirty dress that hung like a loose tent over her morbidly obese body. Her hair was greasy and stringy. She reeked of cigarettes, was missing a front tooth, and her breath was so foul I had to discreetly lean back as she spoke to me. Her grammar was poor and her thought patterns—insofar as I could understand them—were simple. For several minutes she incoherently rambled on about a number of things, seemingly oblivious to the line of people behind her who also wanted to speak with me. My several attempts to help her get to her point, if she had one, fell on deaf ears.

At some point I recognized a person in the line that had formed behind this woman to be the well-known president of a very important and influential ministry. I wanted to meet this man badly, especially since I had an idea about how my church could partner with his ministry. But this lady just kept going on and on! I tried to draw her attention to the fact that there was a line of people waiting behind her, but this seemed not to concern her in the least. I eventually interrupted the woman and told her I had to move on to talk to others, but she simply ignored me and kept talking.

The line began to thin out as people grew tired of waiting, and my own impatience started to turn to anger. I was just about to decide to simply ignore this lady and begin talking to the ministry president who was at this point next in line when, for whatever reason, I suddenly recalled Jesus' teaching that the way we treat "the least of these" is the way we treat *him*. This was immediately followed by a still small voice that whispered, "This lady is my precious daughter and radiant bride. Treat her like the Queen she is."

I instantly realized I'd bought into the cultural lie that people who look, smell, and talk like this lady are less important than people like the president of an influential ministry.

I privately repented of my class judgment and gave the woman my full attention while praying blessings over her in my mind. Whether my blessing prayers helped or whether this lady just ran out of things to talk about, she suddenly got to her point. She wanted money for gas to get home from church.

When I finally managed to speak with the ministry president, far from being flustered from having to wait so long, he was impressed I gave this lady so much time and attention. I explained to him that what looked like virtuous behavior was actually the result of a divine chastisement. When the few folks who remained had been spoken to, I took the Queen and her two kids to a gas station and then out to eat at a local restaurant.

Why did I instinctively judge this woman as being less important than the ministry president? It was because I put her in a different class than the president. I literally *class*-ified her. In doing this, I failed to carry out my central Kingdom duty of manifesting the truth that this woman has unsurpassable worth, for she was worth Jesus' dying for. In my class-ification, this daughter of the King wasn't even worth the same as the ministry president. The truth of who she was got suppressed in my class judgment.

Of course, we who live in American claim to believe that "all people are created equal." America is supposedly "the land of equal opportunity." So we often pretend we don't class-ify people. In fact, we have a long tradition of looking down on societies in which people are born into fixed classes, with some destined from birth to reign as royalty and others to be their servants. But our judgment is somewhat hypocritical, for the fact is that we who live in America have our own class system. We're just less honest about it. Our judgments are so embedded in our usual way of looking at the world that we tend to not even notice them.

WHICH LADY DO YOU NOTICE?

Several years ago the ABC news show *20/20* reported on a sociological study of how perceived beauty affects the ways in which women are treated. The researchers placed two women in a crowded train station at the bottom of a long staircase with a large suitcase. Taking turns, each woman was to act like they were struggling to pull the suitcase up the stairs. The goal was to see how frequently people—especially men—offered to help each woman. The first woman was by customary Western social standards pretty and sexy while the second was average-looking and somewhat overweight.

It took the pretty woman only a couple of seconds before a man offered to help her. It took the average-looking woman several minutes. It was painful to watch. The test was repeated many times, always with the same results. On top of this, the researchers measured the amount of eye contact and verbal exchanges made between the women and their helpers. Not surprisingly, the attention given to the average-looking overweight woman was a small fraction of the attention given to the pretty, sexy woman—and not just by men.

What was even more amazing, however, was that all the helpers of the pretty woman were interviewed as soon as they completed their task and, without exception, each one claimed their decision to help had nothing to do with how this woman looked. They also interviewed a number of people who walked past the average-looking woman struggling to get the suitcase up the stairs, and, without exception, the people claimed they simply didn't notice her.

We tend to be unaware of the ways we instinctively class-ify people.

HOW HE LIVED AND HOW HE DIED

While it's undeniable that we're socially conditioned to class-ify people, this doesn't mean we're *fated* to do so. There is another, more beautiful, way of living and relating to people. It's the way of Jesus.

Jesus manifested the beauty of what it looks like when God reigns in one's life by revolting against all of society's class judgments. He didn't do this by playing politics or by trying to get Caesar to make society fairer. He rather revolted against classism and warred against the Powers that fuel it by how he lived and by how he died.

In first-century Jewish culture, disabled people were often seen as being cursed by God and were therefore often treated as misfits and outcasts. Most had to survive by begging on the street. People with skin diseases were considered unclean and untouchable. Condemned criminals and impoverished people were generally looked down upon as scumbags. Certain kinds of sinners were deemed to constitute an untouchable class. Women were on the whole considered second-class citizens and were generally viewed as property owned by men.

Jesus revolted against this classism by touching lepers, healing the sick, treating beggars as equals, treating women with respect, identifying with the poor, and befriending those judged as the worst sinners. In fact, Jesus taught his followers that how they treat these sorts of people is how they treat him (Matthew 25:35–36, 42–43). In he end, Jesus ascribed unsurpassable worth to each and every one of these marginalized people by giving his life for them.

In living and dying this way, Jesus revolted against every social judgment that oppresses people and revolted against the Powers that fuel this oppression. We who have committed ourselves to following Jesus are commissioned and empowered to do the same.

PROCLAIMING THE YEAR OF JUBILEE

To appreciate how central abolishing class distinctions was to the ministry of Jesus, we need only examine the sermon that launched his ministry. In Luke 4, we find Jesus visiting his hometown synagogue. At one point Jesus stood up and read from Isaiah 61.

> *The Spirit of the Lord is on me,*
> *because he has anointed me*
> *to proclaim good news to the poor.*
> *He has sent me to proclaim freedom for the prisoners*
> *and recovery of sight for the blind,*
> *to set the oppressed free,*
> *to proclaim the year of the Lord's favor.*

Jesus then shocked his fellow townspeople by announcing, "Today this scripture is fulfilled in your hearing."

Most scholars agree this passage refers to the "year of Jubilee" in the Old Testament. Every fifty years all debts were to be cancelled, all land lost through indebtedness was to be restored, and all slaves and prisoners were to be set free. It was, in short, a year in which all inequalities, and thus all class distinctions, were to be abolished.

This was obviously good news to lower class folks—the poor, the enslaved, the lame, the imprisoned, and the oppressed—but bad news to upper class folks who benefited from these social inequalities. It's not too surprising that we have no historical record of this divine command ever being obeyed in ancient Israel.

In this inaugural address, Jesus presented himself as the bringer of this "year of Jubilee." He clearly interpreted the "year" figuratively as referring to the new epoch he was inaugurating with his ministry. He announced that the revolution he came to unleash would be centered on erasing all debts and reversing all class judgments. This is why Jesus taught his followers to not expect repayment when we lend to others, even our enemies. It's why he taught that we're to offer thieves who stole from us more than they took. We're to live in "the year of Jubilee" and, as ludicrous and impractical as it may appear, this is what it looks like.

In the Kingdom, all class judgments are to be erased. We're to make no distinction between rich and poor, male or female, Jew or Gentile, free or slave, good citizen or criminal, able-bodied person or disabled person, holy or unholy. Our lives are to manifest the truth that where God reigns, all class-ifications that assign people pre-established social values are rendered null and void. Where God reigns, people are to be defined solely by what God did for them by dying on Calvary, not by their social class.

Luke goes on to tell us that the townspeople were both amazed at Jesus' "gracious words" and understandably surprised that he applied this teaching to himself. "Isn't this Joseph's son?" they wondered. But then they turned against him—to the point where they wanted him dead.

A closer look at the passage reveals why this happened, and it tells us a great deal about the classless Kingdom Jesus came to establish. Two points are worth mentioning.

AN EPOCH FREE OF JUDGMENT

First, it's significant that Jesus stopped reading and put the scroll down right after he read "the year of the Lord's favor." Had he read the very next line in Isaiah, he would have added "and the day of vengeance of our God." This omission wouldn't have gone unnoticed by his first-century Jewish audience, and it undoubtedly contributed to their offense.

Most first-century Jews were looking for a Messiah who would reveal "the Lord's favor" toward *them* but also bring vengeance on their *enemies*. In fact, the vengeance they expected God to bring on their enemies was a central aspect of the favor they expected the Lord to show them. Their good news was centered on the bad news they anticipated for their enemies. For them, therefore, the punch line of the Isaiah passage was "the day of vengeance of our God." Jesus left this punch line out!

His refusal to apply this clause to describe his own ministry reveals that Jesus didn't view his coming or the movement he came to establish as having anything to do with divine judgment.

Whatever God will do at the end of the age, in this present Jubilee epoch God's favor is toward *everyone*—even toward the enemies of those who consider themselves God's favored people. In this present "year of Jubilee," God's reign is marked by unconditional acceptance and favor, not rejection and vengeance. In this year of the Lord's favor, all social distinctions, including the fundamental distinction between friends and enemies, are to be abolished.

This isn't what people who are heavily invested in seeing themselves as exclusively favored by God and seeing their enemies judged want to hear.

THE INSIDE-OUTSIDE REVERSAL

Second, Jesus went on to remind his audience of the story of Elijah feeding and healing the son of the pagan widow in Sidon as well as the remarkable story of Elijah healing the leprous military captain of the Syrian army—at a time when Israel and Syria were at war with each other.

Why did Jesus bring up these stories at this point? It's because both stories provide examples of God's prophets bypassing Israelites to minister to outsiders and "enemies." In telling these stories Jesus was suggesting that the Good News he's bringing would tend to bypass those who consider themselves insiders and would instead be brought to those whom these people considered outsiders and enemies. In other words, those who consider themselves exclusive insiders will tend to become outsiders, while those who have always been judged as outsiders will tend to become insiders.

The only people excluded from the blessedness of this all-inclusive epoch of divine favor are those who insist that their enemies must be excluded.

The theme of an inside-outside reversal brought about by the year of Jubilee runs throughout Jesus' ministry. As the Kingdom is manifested in the world, Jesus repeatedly taught, the first will be last and the last will be first. The exalted will be brought low, and the lowly will be exalted. The blessed will mourn, and those who mourn will be blessed. The outcasts will feast at the banquet, while the originally invited guests will become outcasts. The sinful tax collector who won't even lift his head to heaven will be justified while the righteous Pharisee who prays and fasts will not. The socially disdained prostitutes and tax collectors will get into heaven before the socially respectable religious leaders. And many who thought they did great things for Jesus will find themselves cast out, while many who didn't know they were doing great things for Jesus will be brought in.

It's important for us to notice that these reversal-teachings are not primarily about what will happen at the end of the age when God judges all humans. Too often Christians have inoculated themselves from the radical implications of Jesus' teachings by making them about what God will do in the future instead of how we're to live *in the present*. The truth is that Jesus' teachings and example are primarily about bringing God's will "on earth as it is in heaven" in the lives of his followers *here and now*. We're now living in the year of Jubilee, so all class distinctions are to be abolished in the community of God's people *now*.

True, human society won't be completely free of its fallen ways of class-ifying people until the end of the age when Christ returns and the Powers are fully defeated. But our job is to revolt against these oppressive categories now and to put on display ahead of time the beauty of God's coming Kingdom.

RELIGIOUS CLASS AND THE CLASSLESS TRIBE

Let's begin to bring this home by asking: To what extent is the Western church today living out the year of Jubilee inaugurated by Jesus Christ? To what extent are we manifesting the truth that "in Christ" there is no longer any male or female, Jew or Gentile, free person or slave? To what extent is the Church an all-inclusive, classless tribe of Kingdom people?

We should first celebrate the fact that there are an increasing number of beautiful Jubilee communities springing up in Western countries, including America. If you attend the Dream Center in Los Angeles, for example, you'll find a marvelous countercultural mix of people. You'll see people who would by normal social standards be seen as "upper class" in community with people who by these same standards would be considered "lower class." You'll find wealthy people fellowshipping (and sharing) with poor people. You'll find a community in which people with disabilities are not only being accommodated but also embraced and set free in ministry. You'll find a ministry in which criminals are being visited in prison and then cared for and transformed once they're released. You'll find an environment where struggling prostitutes, drug addicts, sex addicts, and others are considered no different from struggling greedy people, gossipers, gluttons, and self-righteous religious people.

There are, thankfully, many such Jubilee-looking ministries springing up around the world.

At the same time, if we're honest, we have to admit that the Western church as a whole still has a long way to go. It's my impression, at least, that we Christians in America tend to class-ify people at least as much as the broader American culture.

The majority of American churches are as segregated along socioeconomic lines as much as they are along racial lines. Relatively few churches make any effort to welcome, embrace, and equip for ministry people with disabilities. So too, comparatively few Western Christians treat their finances with the reckless abandon required by Jubilee living. We don't generally live as though all debts and obligations owed us have been erased.

Not only this, but in many churches the elderly and prisoners tend to be neglected, despite specific biblical commands to care for them. Many churches continue to restrict the role of women in ministry, as though it was God's timeless will that women remain within the patriarchal constraints of the first century. The majority of evangelical churches continue to rank people with certain types of sins as further from the Kingdom than people with "more accept-able sins" (like the good, all-American sins of greed, gluttony, and judgmentalism). And a good percentage of American Christians seem to hate their enemies, especially their national and religious enemies, at least as much as other Americans tend to hate them.

So, it's certainly no overstatement to say we have a long way to go. We need to hear, again and again, that in the revolution Jesus unleashed on the world, the insider-outsider way of class-ifying people has been completely abolished. The Kingdom has a center—Jesus Christ—but no clearly defined parameters. With reckless abandon, therefore, we are to manifest God's unconditional love by ascribing unsurpassable worth to all people at all times in all conditions.

Whether they are by "normal" social standards upper class or lower class, intelligent or cognitively challenged, educated or uned-ucated, attractive or unattractive, decent or indecent, able-bodied or disabled, male or female, talented or untalented, famous or infa-mous, young or old—our primary job, following Jesus' example, is to manifest the truth that each and every one of these people has unsurpassable worth, as evidenced by the fact that Jesus died for them just as he died for us. And we manifest this truth by how we welcome and embrace them, just as they are.

As we do this, we will manifest the beauty of God's classless Kingdom and revolt against the ugly oppression of all social class-ifications and the Powers that fuel this oppression.

Viva la revolution!

CHAPTER 10

THE REVOLT
AGAINST RACISM

His purpose was to create in himself one new humanity . . .
thus making peace . . .

EPHESIANS 2:15

SEVERAL YEARS AGO I WAS LISTENING TO A CHRISTIAN RADIO TALK show that was discussing the issue of "racial profiling." It was in response to a recent study that determined that in Minnesota (the "liberal" North) black men were much more likely to be stopped in their cars by police than white men. The white host of the show expressed his opinion (citing no evidence) that the study was flawed and that racial profiling was "in fact" very rare. He then took calls from the audience.

The arrogance of the talk show host amused me. But the next half hour of call-ins left me dumbfounded.

One caller early on identified himself as black. He gave two examples from his own life of being pulled over and questioned by police for no legitimate reason. He also mentioned that a number of his black friends had similar experiences. Not surprisingly, while he said he believed most white police officers tried to be fair and that few were consciously racist, he nevertheless felt that racial profiling was a significant problem in the Minnesota police force.

All the remaining callers identified themselves as white, and without exception, each denied racial profiling was a problem. Some even expressed anger toward the black caller for suggesting otherwise. Several said they were sick and tired of nonwhite people "playing the race card."

Now suppose, for the sake of argument, that the study was accurate and that racial profiling is in fact a real problem in Minnesota. How would any of the white callers know about it? By definition, it wouldn't be happening to them. The only way white people could learn about racial profiling would be to learn about it from those who actually get profiled. Yet this was the very thing the white callers on the station were unwilling to do. Instead, because racial profiling never happened to *them*, they insisted it doesn't happen to *anyone*.

In this chapter we're going to see that racial reconciliation lies at the heart of what the Church is supposed to be about. It's arguably the aspect of the Kingdom the Church in America fails at the most. And one of the reasons why, we'll see, has to do with the sort of racial arrogance illustrated on this radio program.

THIS IS AS CENTRAL AS IT GETS

According to the Bible, God created only one race—the human race. The idea that there are different races of humans is a myth created by white Europeans in the eighteenth and nineteenth centuries to justify oppressing and enslaving nonwhites.[1] God's goal has always been that the one human race would be united in a way that reflects the perfect loving union of the Trinity. Unfortunately, our sin caused us to be divided into different factions that are now identified as different races. But as we saw in chapter 7, throughout the Bible God spoke of a time when every tribe and every nation would be reunited under his loving Lordship.

Jesus perfectly embodied God's heart for racial reconciliation. For example, most Jews of Jesus' day despised Samaritans as racially impure and as heretics. They avoided physical or social contact with them if at all possible. Yet Jesus went out of his way to have contact with them, even touching some who were lepers. Moreover, he consistently treated them with respect, even making them the heroes in some of his stories.[2]

Similarly, most Jews of Jesus' day looked down on Gentiles and had a particular disdain for the Romans, the group who ruled Palestine. Yet Jesus treated them as equals. Most remarkably, Jesus was willing to interact with and serve Roman centurions. These were high-ranking officials in the oppressive Roman military and were thus despised by Jews. Jesus went so far as to praise the faith of a Roman centurion as being greater than the faith of any Jew (Matthew 8:5–11)!

This sort of behavior was absolutely scandalous and revolutionary. It reveals that where God reigns, the Powers that fuel racism will be confronted and racial walls will be torn down. Where God reigns, God's vision for a united human race will be in the process of being reconciled.

We see this even more profoundly in Jesus' death. The most fundamental ethnic divide in the ancient world, at least from a Jewish perspective, was the divide between Jews and Gentiles. But by his work on the cross, Paul says, Jesus destroyed the "dividing wall of hostility" between these two groups — and by extension, between all ethnic groups.

Not only has Jesus *brought* peace to all previously hostile groups; he himself *is* the peace between these groups. For through his death Jesus created "one new humanity."

> *He himself is our peace, who has made the two [Jew and Gentile] one and has destroyed the barrier, the dividing wall of hostility.... His purpose was to create in himself one new humanity out of the two, thus making peace, and in one body to reconcile both of them to God through the cross, by which he put to death their hostility. (Ephesians 2:14–16)*

This means that revolting against racism is not a nice addendum to the Gospel, as many contemporary white Christians seem to think. It's one of the reasons Jesus came and died on the cross. It's as central to the Gospel as anything could possibly be. We can no more refrain from proclaiming and demonstrating the reunification of humanity in Christ than we can refrain from preaching forgiveness of sin in Christ!

THE FAILURE
OF THE CONTEMPORARY AMERICAN CHURCH

But let's get honest. How many churches in America are as passionate about proclaiming that Jesus died for racial reconciliation as they are about proclaiming that Jesus died for the forgiveness of sins? The answer, tragically, is relatively few.

What makes this even more tragic is that, as is often pointed out, Sunday morning is the most segregated time in America. Fifty years after the Civil Rights Movement, the Church remains the *least* racially integrated institution in the country. In other words, the broader secular culture generally does a better job of reflecting the coming Kingdom than we Christians do.

Some try to minimize this travesty by claiming that it's just "natural" for people from different races and cultures to worship with "their own people." In fact, some leading church-growth experts have taught what's called the "homogeneous church growth" principle. The most effective way of building a church, they say, is to aim at building it around a single homogenous people-group. They point out that it's generally harder to get people to join a church if it's racially and culturally diverse.

I don't doubt that this is true. But when did Jesus ever call us to be comfortable or encourage us to make nonbelievers comfortable in order to get them to accept the Gospel? And when did Jesus ever call us to be focused on growing large churches?

The answer is, never.

To the contrary, Jesus was perfectly willing to make people profoundly *uncomfortable* and to let people walk away when they understood the high cost of following him. His one and only concern was to be obedient to his Father's will, not to be efficient at acquiring a large following. And since we are called to imitate him in all things, this must be our one concern as well.

We are called to manifest the "one new humanity" Jesus died to create — whether it makes people comfortable or not, and whether it increases or decreases the size of our congregations.

THE CHALLENGE OF RACIAL RECONCILIATION

Getting people to relinquish their racist attitudes is profoundly difficult — especially because most aren't even aware they have any. This isn't just a modern problem. It existed in the early church.

For example, despite Jesus' command to take the Gospel to all nations, we find his disciples in the book of Acts still hanging around Jerusalem in the nice Jewish environment in which they were most comfortable years after his ascension. It took an explicit vision from God and coaching by some *pagans* for Peter to finally realize that "God does not show favoritism" and that God wanted to incorporate Gentiles into the "one new humanity" Jesus died to create (Acts 10).

Not surprisingly, the first major conflict the early church had to work through centered on race relations (Acts 15). The issue concerned how Gentile and Jewish Christians could get along with each other. But even after this was worked out, racist attitudes persisted. For example, Paul had to rebuke Peter for succumbing to the segregationist eating practices of some fellow Jews (Galatians 2:12 – 14).

Tearing down racial walls was difficult for early Christians and it's difficult today. Yet if our commitment to Christ is genuine, we have no choice but to passionately embrace this challenge.

THE MAIN OBSTACLE
(ACCORDING TO THIS AMERICAN WHITE GUY)

I now need to confront what is, I believe, the biggest obstacle to manifesting the "one new humanity" in America today.[3] In confronting this I have to acknowledge up front that I'm a white guy (of a Scottish-Irish-wee-bit-French variety). This colors my perspective on this (and every other) issue. Whenever we enter into discussions about race it's important to acknowledge the limitations of our own cultural perspective and life experience. When we fail to do this, we easily end up canonizing our limited perspective as the norm and thus dismissing differing perspectives as defective. And this, we'll now see, only serves to keep us divided from those whose perspectives differ from our own.

The most difficult challenge I've found as I've tried to lead a congregation that aspires to manifest the "one new humanity" of the Kingdom is that many white people honestly don't see racial reconciliation as that big of an issue. They seem to think it's a problem America has largely overcome.

Of course they know about racist groups like the Ku Klux Klan or the Aryan Nation, and they're naturally opposed to them. And once in a while they hear about the overtly racist behavior of a police officer or the stupid racist comments made by some radio talk show host, and they object to this. The trouble is, this is all that many white people think racism amounts to.

The truth is, racism in America is far more subtle and sinister than this. America was conquered by white Europeans, was structured by and for white Europeans, and it continues to privilege white Europeans. Racism has been woven into the very fabric of our culture from the start.

This racism was obvious when many of our white founding fathers proclaimed the "manifest destiny" doctrine, asserting that it was God's will for them to conquer and rule nonwhite people. It was obvious when white Europeans acquired America's land by cheating and slaughtering its indigenous population while accumulating incredible wealth by the forced labor of millions of African slaves. It continued to be obvious even after the Civil War when whites imposed "Jim Crow" laws that blocked blacks and other nonwhites from acquiring significant power, privilege, and opportunities.

Despite the fact that we have a black president, this racism continues today, as most nonwhites will testify. It's just that it's no longer obvious to most whites. One of the ways the social system of America continues to privilege whites over others is that it insulates us from the ongoing effects of America's racist past.

And this is why many sincere white people fail to see why racial reconciliation is a big deal.

If the church in America is going to make progress in manifesting the "one new humanity" of the Kingdom, this obstacle has to be overcome.

THE HIERARCHY OF PRIVILEGE

Sixteen years ago when I helped plant the church I now pastor, I naively thought that if I simply taught that reconciliation is central to the Gospel our church would quickly become a diverse, multi-ethnic congregation. I was baffled when our church remained 98 percent white five years into the ministry.

I now understand why. My perspective on the world and my way of doing church were entirely white. While I had many acquaintances who were nonwhite, I had no deep friendships that enabled me to genuinely "get on the inside" of other cultures and appreciate how different they are from my own. As a result, I didn't realize that, while we *said* we welcomed all people, we were actually requiring people to check their nonwhite culture at the door and join our "white" way of doing church.

Even more importantly, because I wasn't "on the inside" of the nonwhite experience of American culture, I naively assumed my "white" experience was pretty much "the norm." I was largely unaware of the systemic racism that continues to permeate American culture. I was oblivious to the fact that I, as a white person, sat at the top of a hierarchy of privilege that allowed me to hover freely above thick but largely invisible walls that restrict opportunities for nonwhites.

Over time I've developed honest, trusting relationships with nonwhites. Sharing experiences with these friends has opened my eyes to a hierarchy of privilege that advantages me and disadvantages them. I envision this hierarchy something like the diagram on the following page.

The walls that restrict others are invisible to most whites because we never have to run up against them. It's why the whites who called in on the radio talk show could so easily dismiss the study that exposed racial profiling. It's why whites can honestly

The Hierarchy of Privilege

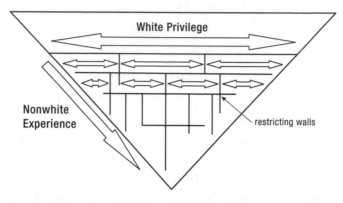

believe the slogan that America is a "land of equal opportunity," despite the fact that all the evidence indicates that it is not.

Why are whites three times more likely to own homes, four times more likely to earn a college degree, and five times less likely to end up in prison than African Americans? Why do whites tend to earn significantly more and own significantly more than non-whites? Why are most of the top positions in major corporations occupied by white males?

Faced with statistics like this, many whites simply appeal to individual choices. "People choose to commit crimes and so end up in prison rather than in college. It's that simple."

Well, it's *not* "that simple." Of course every individual must take responsibility for his or her actions—but individual choices alone don't explain group behavior. To understand why the group experiences of whites and nonwhites differ so radically—and why whites happen to usually "come out on top"—we have to understand the ongoing destructive effects of America's racist past. And the most important effect to consider is the hierarchy of privilege we've inherited and that we who are white continue to benefit from, usually without knowing it.

If followers of Jesus in America are going to make progress manifesting the "one new humanity" of the Kingdom, this system of privilege must be acknowledged and revolted against.

LISTENING, LEARNING, AND FOLLOWING

In this light, I believe the first step to manifesting the "one new humanity" Jesus died to create is for whites to humbly acknowledge that we don't know what we don't know. The only way we can possibly learn about the walls we are privileged to hover above is by listening to the life experiences of those who run into them.

So, for example, rather than normalizing our own (privileged) experience and thus denying that racial profiling exists—accusing all who claim otherwise of "playing the race card"—we who are white must humbly listen to and trust the experience of nonwhites whose experience suggest that it does.

To wake up to the systemic racism of our culture, we who are white need to cultivate relationships with nonwhites that are deep enough to allow us to "get on the inside" of a nonwhite experience of the world. Not only this, but where it is appropriate, we who are white need to submit to the leadership of nonwhites. Individuals, small groups, and predominately white churches must pursue these submitted relationships if we're to make headway in manifesting "the one new humanity." I've become convinced that, as helpful as books and seminars on racism are, they are in most cases not enough to bring about permanent changes in the way white people view the world. On this matter, whites need people of color to teach us and to lead us.

This is frankly challenging for many whites, even for those who sincerely believe they want to be agents of reconciliation. Our privileged status has conditioned us to assume our perspectives are normative and to expect to have things our way. Because America was established by and for whites, nonwhites have to deal with *our* culture, but we don't usually have to deal with *theirs*. The decision to listen, learn, and follow people of color requires whites to place themselves in a submitted position they aren't accustomed to. But if the systemic racism that has characterized the American church throughout its history is going to be subverted, this is the first step that must be taken.

AN EXAMPLE OF BLOWING IT

About three years after Woodland Hills Church started, we asked an African American man named Norm Blagman to be our worship leader. Norm was a relatively new Christian and had no background in leading worship, but the man is (no exaggeration) a musical genius. He has the equivalent of a photographic memory when it comes to music. He can hear a song once and then ten years later recall what every instrument and voice does in the song. He can also sing and play congas like nobody's business. And most importantly, Norm has a passion and gift for worship leading.

About six months after Norm joined our otherwise exclusively white pastoral staff, a young white man in our congregation began to persistently write letters and leave voice messages for Norm and myself about a number of theological matters that bothered him. Among other things, this man thought it was unbiblical and offensive that Norm sometimes wore a cap while leading worship. In several of his contacts with Norm he made reference to "you people," which Norm took to mean, "You black people." (I've since learned that "you people" is often used by whites to stereotype blacks.)

Over several months Norm expressed his concern that this guy's behavior was at least partly racially motivated and that he saw trouble brewing. He suggested—and then pleaded—that I and others in leadership do something to address this problem before it grew into something bigger. Instead of humbly following Norm's lead on this, I encouraged him to just ignore the guy. In my view the man was crazy, but not a racist. After all, I was getting more letters and phone calls than Norm, and most of this man's messages were bizarre ramblings about end-time prophecies or megalomaniac pronouncements about how he was God's anointed prophet. The issue of Norm's cap, in my view, was almost incidental.

So I told Norm that in large churches like ours we should expect to occasionally have to deal with crazy people. Norm was new to ministry, and I was just trying to toughen him up for the years of ministry he had ahead of him.

Well, my advice didn't help. Norm's concern grew to the point where he asked me and other pastors to consider getting a restraining order barring this guy from church and from contacting Norm. I agreed to meet with the man and tell him to stop hassling us, but everyone in leadership except Norm thought that taking out a restraining order on a man who hadn't made any threats was unwarranted. "You just have to learn how to deal graciously with crazy people like this," we kept telling Norm.

Then, several weeks after this, the disturbed man confronted Norm after one of our church services. He pushed a lady to the floor and shoved a Bible in Norm's face while screaming something about how Norm wasn't fit to be a worship leader. Norm instinctively responded by pushing the man back and pinning him up against the wall. There was a crowd of parishioners around who intervened to break up the altercation.

When the pastoral staff processed the event the next day, it was decided that we needed to take out a restraining order on the disturbed man. It was also decided that Norm, being a pastor, needed to confess to the congregation that he had "lost his cool" and that he should not have responded to this man so forcefully.

At the time—and for a good while after this event—I felt like we handled the episode pretty much "by the book." The problem, I now see, is that the "book" we were going by was written exclusively by, and for, white people.

Here's the side of the story our "white book" didn't include.

Norm was raised in a New York City ghetto, and like many other inner-city black youth, his early life experience and social conditioning led him to have a certain mistrust of white people—especially white people in positions of power. Over the years Norm had several experiences working in white establishments that reinforced this mistrust. Among other things, he found that white bosses tended to believe white employees and customers over black employees and customers. So, whenever a white employee or customer raised an issue with him, Norm found his job was on the line—regardless of how frivolous the complaint may have been.

I lacked the capacity to appreciate this at the time, but I now understand that it took tremendous courage for Norm to accept a leadership position in a church that was almost completely white and run by all white people. The question on his mind was, "Will the white leadership of this church believe me and cover my back if a white person in the congregation raises an issue about me?"

This question was put to the test when the disturbed white man began raising the issue over Norm's cap. As a white person who never had to worry about losing my job for frivolous racial reasons, it was easy for me to dismiss the man as just another example of the kind of disturbed people pastors sometimes have to put up with. But as a black person who had lost several jobs for just such reasons, it was not so easy for Norm.

Indeed, my well-intentioned advice to Norm that he adopt a dismissive attitude toward this man actually intensified his worry that, if push came to shove (no pun intended), the white leadership of this church would not believe him or cover his back. Norm rightly discerned that his black perspective on this issue was simply not being taken seriously.

When the disturbed man aggressively accosted him after a church service, Norm felt like he had felt so often in his life: he was completely on his own in a white-run organization. No one believed him, and so he felt he had no option except to take matters into his own hands and defend himself. He later told me he felt like a wounded badger backed into a corner.

While it helped that we (finally) got a restraining order against the man, the fact that Norm had to publicly apologize to the congregation reinforced this sense of aloneness. Far from feeling like he was believed and understood, he felt like he was once again being made out to be the bad guy. It's true that Norm didn't model Christ's teaching on turning the other cheek in the way he responded to his aggressor. But had we listened to Norm, matters never would have come to this. We failed Norm.

Now, I'll admit that it took me several years of being friends with Norm and working through a number of difficult race-related issues before I could fully empathize with Norm's perspective of this episode. I now realize that, as sincere as my intentions were, I, and the rest of the white leadership of the church, responded to this event poorly. Sitting at the top of the hierarchy of privilege, I was simply unaware of the radically different world in which Norm lived. I responded to this event from a strictly white perspective rather than allowing my perspective to be stretched by Norm and humbly following his lead on this issue.

I now try to humbly listen, learn, and follow when I need to. This doesn't mean I consider a nonwhite perspective to always be right while mine is automatically wrong if we see things differently. But it does mean I try to remain open to the possibility that our disagreement may be due to the fact that our lives have been conditioned by where we're positioned in the hierarchy of privilege.

Reconciliation is profoundly difficult even with a full awareness of the hierarchy of privilege and the historical and social influences that have constructed it. But without this awareness and without a willingness to listen, learn, and follow, it's not even remotely possible. Without this awareness, many sincere, well-intentioned white believers won't even see that there's a problem that needs to be overcome.

RECONCILIATION FOR ALL PEOPLE

So far my comments have been directed entirely toward white readers. The reason for this is that I believe the main obstacle to reconciliation in the body of Christ in America is that most whites don't really see a need for it, as I said above. Not only this, but as a white person I can only address this (and every other) issue from a white perspective.

Still, the call to be a reconciled and reconciling community applies to *all* Kingdom people, so we need to address what reconciliation looks like for non-European, nonwhite Americans. Here I have had to rely entirely on insights from my nonwhite sisters and brothers. There are three things that need to be said.

First, I encourage people of color to embrace Paul's teaching that the Kingdom struggle is never against "flesh and blood" but against the Powers. We conquer them by refusing to hate, choosing instead to follow Jesus' example of extending outrageous, self-sacrificial love to all people—even those who are intentionally or unintentionally oppressing us.

Second, it's important for people of color to extend forgiveness, both for things done to their ethnic group in the past and for things that continue to be done in the present. Jesus reflected the attitude Kingdom people are to have when he prayed for our forgiveness before we ever dreamed of asking for it. Only this kind of love can tear down the hostile walls that have been built up over centuries and empower us to manifest the "one new humanity" Christ died to create.

Third, Kingdom reconciliation is impossible without Kingdom relationships. I therefore encourage people of color as well as white people to revolt against our tribal instincts to remain in the security of our own ethnic group and actively pursue relationships with people whose ethnicity is different than our own. Cross-ethnic relationships are, by their very nature, revolting against Powers that have installed and aggravated mistrust between different ethnic groups for centuries. Racial reconciliation is spiritual warfare, so we must not naively think forging such relationships is going to be easy. But they *are* always worth it.

THE UNIQUENESS OF KINGDOM RECONCILIATION

The world's way of achieving racial reconciliation focuses on equalizing power and privilege. It tends to have an adversarial quality to it as those with less power and privilege confront those who have more. A central goal is to achieve a fairer society. This is a good and necessary endeavor in the broader society, and all fair-minded people should obviously pursue it.

Reconciliation in the Kingdom looks very different from this, however. Our focus is not on equalizing power and privilege; it's on following the example of Jesus by abandoning the quest for power and privilege. Our goal is not to achieve more fairness; it's to manifest Christlike submission to one another. And our adversaries are not other people who have more power and privilege than ourselves. Our adversaries are the Powers who keep humanity in bondage by fueling our hunger for power and privilege while enforcing social structures that give more to some by robbing it from others.

Our Kingdom call is to revolt against the Powers by dismantling the hierarchy of privilege, rejecting all racial stereotypes and judgments, forging meaningful relationships across ethnic lines, and submitting ourselves to one another as we listen, learn, and follow one another.

As we do this, we participate in the Kingdom that Jesus unleashed into the world. It's a revolution that manifests the beauty of God's dream for a united humanity while revolting against all forms of racism and the ugly Powers that fuel it.

Viva la revolution!

CHAPTER 11

THE REVOLT AGAINST POVERTY AND GREED

Each one of them is Jesus in disguise.

MOTHER TERESA

Greed is a bottomless pit which exhausts the person in an endless effort
to satisfy the need without ever reaching satisfaction.

ERICH FROMM

MEET "THE RICH"

Some time ago I got into an animated conversation with a man who
I knew had sacrificed a good deal to live in solidarity with the poor.
At one point he claimed, "There's no way a Christian living in a
two-million-dollar home can say they're following Jesus' example
of self-sacrificial living."

"Really?" I said. "How about a million-dollar house, or a quarter-
of-a-million-dollar house? Or how about a little run-down fifty-
thousand-dollar house?" I asked. "After all, such a house would
be considered a mansion by a large percent of people around the
globe."

The man smiled because he was aware that I knew this was
about what his house cost—and he was feeling a bit self-righteous
about it.

When we hear about Jesus' teaching on the dangers of wealth
and the evils of greed, I'm guessing many of us assume the teaching applies to other people, not ourselves. We tend to identify "the
rich" as those who have more than we have. Few people identify
themselves as rich, let alone greedy.

By global and historical standards, however, the majority of us in Western countries are rich—extremely rich. Only the wealthiest people throughout history had anything close to the standard of living middle class westerners enjoy today. When Jesus offers warnings to "the rich," therefore, he's talking about most of us. And his warning is that riches have a way of entrapping us.

All indications are that most Americans have become entrapped in wealth. Studies have shown that the wealthier people become, the lower percentage of their income they tend to give away. For example, in 2000 the gap between the average wealth of Americans and that of the poorest 25 percent of people on the planet was four times greater than what it had been in 1960. During this same period of time, the percentage of our country's GNP (Gross National Product) that went to providing assistance to the poorest 25 percent of people on the planet *decreased* to about one tenth of what it had been in 1960.[1] While there are many incredibly generous Americans, as a nation we've clearly become entrapped by our wealth.

It's sobering to compare America's spending on the military with its aid to the poor. In 2005 America spent twenty-seven times more on its military than it did on alleviating global poverty. Some estimate that the amount spent on the Iraq war alone in 2006 could have fed and housed all the poor on the planet six times over. Its also sobering to consider that Americans spend enough money on entertainment each year to feed all the hungry people on the planet for a year.

What does God think about all this?

JESUS, THE POOR, AND THE GREEDY

There are literally thousands of passages in the Bible in which God warns against greed (hoarding more than you need) and in which he emphasizes the need for his people to share with the poor. In fact, the number one reason given in the Bible for why God brings judgment on nations is that they hoard food and wealth and neglect the plight of the poor. Not surprisingly the condemnation of greed and call to care for the poor also permeates the life and teaching of Jesus.

Jesus gave us an example to follow when he set aside the riches of his divine status and entered into solidarity with the poor. "Though he was rich," Paul said, "he made himself poor." Followers of Jesus who are wealthy by global and historical standards (most of us Americans) are to consider the poor our sisters and brothers whom we are responsible for.

Jesus repeatedly stressed the danger of riches and the need to live generously. He criticized the religious heroes of his day for being preoccupied with maintaining a nice religious exterior while their hearts were full of "greed and wickedness." These people meticulously followed religious rules, but because they loved money they "neglected the more important matters of the law," which include "justice" and "mercy." In other words, their religious appearance notwithstanding, these people consumed and hoarded resources and didn't share with the poor. Clearly, in Jesus' view, this omission rendered the rest of their religious behavior irrelevant.

Along the same lines, when a man wanted Jesus to settle a legal dispute with his older brother over how much of the family inheritance he should receive, Jesus said, "Man, who appointed me a judge or an arbiter between you?" He was basically asking the man, "Do I *look* like your lawyer?" Jesus hadn't come to settle legal and political problems. He had rather come to manifest the reign of God and revolt against everything that is inconsistent with it— including things like greed. So Jesus warned the man, "Watch out. Be on your guard against all kinds of greed; life does not consist in an abundance of possessions."

"However you work out your legal and political issues," Jesus was in essence saying, "make sure you're not being motivated by greed."

Jesus taught that while pagans naturally chase after material things, Kingdom people are to remain worry free as we trust our heavenly Father to provide for us. He repeatedly warned that those who try to store up treasures on earth and neglect the poor will face

God's judgment. By contrast, Jesus told his followers they weren't to consider anything they own as their possessions. "Those of you who do not give up everything you have cannot be my disciples," he said. Since we have no possessions, we're to share all we own with everyone in need.

When we throw a banquet, Jesus says, "invite the poor, the crippled, the lame, the blind." Then "you will be blessed," he says, for these people "cannot repay you"—but God most certainly will. If we come upon anyone in need, we're to follow his example of "the good Samaritan" and offer what we have to help them. Even if our enemy is in need, Jesus taught, we're to share what we have with them. According to the New Testament, we can't claim to love God if we ignore the basic needs of people around us. James says that anyone who ignores the needs of the poor has a faith that is "dead."

LIVING WITH OUTRAGEOUS GENEROSITY

If you've been conditioned by the typical, Western consumer mindset, the example of Jesus and the teachings of the New Testament regarding our responsibility to share with the poor may feel impossibly onerous. We're conditioned to think that living with as much luxury and convenience as possible—attaining "the American dream"—is what life is all about. Whatever we may theoretically believe about God, Jesus, and the Kingdom of God, we're conditioned to instinctively try to find our happiness, worth, and security in things.

Not only this, but we're conditioned to feel as though we never have enough. The average American watches over 20,000 commercials each year and almost every single one of them is designed to convince us we *need* whatever's being sold. For all of its economic advantages, capitalism thrives on people remaining discontented with what they have. If the American population as a whole ever adhered to Paul's instruction to be content with what we already have (1 Timothy 6:8–9), our economy would collapse overnight.

And so, like the pagans of old that Jesus talked about—but undoubtedly with a much greater consumer vengeance—we westerners tend to addictively chase after things. Held in bondage to our consumer conditioning, the biblical teaching to own nothing and to sacrificially give to the poor may feel like absolute torture.

The truth is that the Kingdom call to live without possessions and with outrageous generosity is a call to *freedom*. While the Powers delude us into believing that possessing things gives us Life, the truth is that whatever we think we possess actually possesses us. The truth is that owning things doesn't give Life; it sucks Life out of us. The truth is that the perpetual hunger for more that fuels capitalism is a form of demonic bondage.

We never experience more joy, and never feel more fully alive, than when we are sacrificially sharing with others. Possessing things may bring momentary happiness, but only sacrificing for others can bring true, lasting joy. The paradox of the Kingdom—and it applies to all of life—is that the best thing we can do for ourselves is to decide *not* to live for ourselves.

BEWARE OF GUILT AND JUDGMENT

Some who become aware of the massive discrepancy between their comfortable Western standard of living and the deplorable standard of living of the world's poorest people become ridden with guilt. Judging from the statistics about how most Americans spend their money—98 percent of it on themselves—there's no question that most of us Americans *should* feel guilty about our self-indulgent lifestyles. At the same time, we need to be very clear that guilt is not a Kingdom motivation for sacrificial giving.

We're supposed to be imitators of God in all things. God didn't set aside his advantages and enter into solidarity with us out of guilt. He did it out of love. So too, Paul says, everything followers of Jesus do is to be motivated by love.

When a person sacrifices for the poor out of guilt, it's very easy for them to project their guilt onto people who haven't made the sacrifices they've made and to become judgmental. Honestly, some of the most judgmental people I've ever met have been people who have walked away from comfort and convenience to enter into solidarity with the poor. They developed a disdain for people who haven't made the sacrifices they've made. Several I've known have become so judgmental they've sunk into a hole of cynicism toward the Church, and even toward Christianity as a whole.

Our job as Kingdom people is to obey what God calls *us* to do, not judge others concerning whether or not *they* are doing what God calls them to do. As each servant answers to their own master, Paul says, each person must answer to God on their own. If we're in a covenant community with another who has invited us to hold them accountable, then it is appropriate to be concerned with how they steward their resources. But outside of this sort of relationship, our only job is to agree with God that each person we see—however rich and self-indulgent they may appear to us—has unsurpassable worth, as demonstrated by the unsurpassable sacrifice God was willing to make for them.

Related to this, while all Kingdom people are called to live sacrificial lives and share with the poor, the particular way we do this must flow out of our sense of what God is telling us and our community of fellow disciples to do. It can't flow out of a set of ethical rules about wealth that we think apply to all Christians at all times.

There are no such rules. There is no absolute standard against which we can assess whether another individual is giving "enough" or not. The same judgmental logic that would rule out a two-million-dollar home could also rule out a fifty-thousand-dollar home. In fact, as long as a person has *anything* another doesn't have, one could accuse them of not caring enough about the poor.

The call of the Kingdom is not to create rules that we think everyone should conform to. It's simply to seek God's will as to how he would have us live out Jesus' self-sacrificial lifestyle.

WHERE SHOULD WE PLACE OUR TRUST?

In the same way that the Kingdom call to serve the poor can't be reduced to a set of rules about wealth, it also can't be identified with any political or economic program to rid the world of poverty. Kingdom people have no special wisdom about these things, for the New Testament is silent about such matters.

This isn't to say that governments shouldn't help relieve poverty or that Christians shouldn't sometimes help them do it. Sometimes they can, and sometimes we should. Any clever political ideas about how people and resources can be better mobilized to relieve hunger and poverty are to be welcomed and, if proven effective, embraced.

But our confidence as Kingdom people should be rooted not in smart political and economic programs, but in God, who promises to use our individual and collective sacrifices to revolt against, and ultimately overthrow, poverty and the Powers that fuel it. Hence, our primary time and energy should be invested not in debating the relative merits of competing political and economic programs, but in individually and collectively imitating Jesus by bleeding for people who are in need.

If significant numbers of Kingdom people lived like this, it would in fact be politically revolutionary. But it would be so in a way that looks like Jesus rather than Caesar.

Along these same lines, it's crucial we remember that the criteria for success in the Kingdom is not effectiveness, but faithfulness. Our job is to obediently "plant" and "water" as God leads us. It's God's job to "give the increase."

Jesus made this point one day while he and his disciples observed wealthy people putting huge offerings into the temple treasury. They then saw a "poor widow" put in "two very small copper coins." Jesus told his disciples, "This poor widow has put in more than all the others." The reason was that the wealthy people "gave their gifts out of their wealth" while the widow "out of her poverty put in all she had to live on."

The world would certainly be more impressed with a thousand dollars dropped in an offering plate than with two pennies. Obviously you can do a lot more with a thousand dollars than with two pennies, right? Yet Jesus tells us we're not to assess things this way, for in the Kingdom what matters is not how *much* one gives, but how much it *cost* one to give it. The widow gave all she had and thus advanced the Kingdom more than all the wealthy folks whose gifts were larger but didn't cost them as much to give.

So too, our confidence in addressing poverty must not be in things the world thinks are effective but in what God can do when people faithfully imitate Jesus and make costly sacrifices for the poor.

KNOWING WHAT YOU ARE —
AND ARE NOT — RESPONSIBLE FOR

While most American disciples need to be challenged to assume more responsibility for the poor, some need to be challenged to assume *less*. I'm serious. It's a lesson I had to learn the hard way.

My first visit to Haiti twelve years ago was emotionally and spiritually overwhelming. I knew the statistics about poverty in Haiti, but knowing about dehumanizing poverty and experiencing it are two very different things.

Cité Soleil, a seaside slum, exists on about one square mile of garbage-infested land and is home to over a quarter million people. It's among the most impoverished places on earth. As we were driving through Cité Soleil, at one point I caught the eyes of a young child rummaging through a three-foot-high pile of filthy, smelly garbage, looking for food. He glanced up as our van passed, and for a timeless moment our eyes were locked on each other.

I was immediately overwhelmed with grief and jolted by an acute sense of how grotesquely arbitrary life is. There was absolutely no reason why I was *me* instead of *this* boy, I thought. Nothing but sheer luck allowed me to be born in a nice American home rather than in this stench-filled Haitian dump. Nothing but sheer luck placed me inside this air-conditioned van looking out rather than on that smelly pile of garbage looking in. The absurdity of the situation made me feel nauseated.

I couldn't get this sense of absurdity out of my mind once I returned home. I saw this boy's malnourished face on every dollar bill. Whenever I was going to purchase anything, I wondered, "Is this purchase more important than feeding a Haitian child?" And of course, the answer was almost always no. If I purchased the item anyway, I felt like I was virtually killing a starving child!

That dollar could have been used to feed him.

For close to a year I had trouble spending money on anything that wasn't absolutely essential: movies, nice meals, new clothes, even Christmas presents for my own children. I began to loathe American culture as a whole and despise my own participation in it. I fell into a black hole of cynicism.

This wasn't particularly helpful to my marriage. My wife rarely buys things we don't need, but her standard of "need" is a bit higher than it is for people in Cité Soleil. One time my poor wife wanted to replace the old shabby curtains in our living room. They really were in pretty bad shape. But my response was, "How many kids will go without food because we chose to buy curtains rather than feed them?"

It wasn't the happiest year of our marriage.

I slowly realized I was shouldering far more responsibility than God had given me, and it was crushing me. Certainly those of us who are privileged by wealth have a responsibility to steward our advantages in ways that help the disadvantaged. But what I had forgotten was that, as a Kingdom person, I am to seek God's will about how I'm supposed to do this. I'm not to assume responsibility for every impoverished child in Haiti. I'm to assume responsibility only for those God entrusts to me.

When I sought God's will, I came to believe the Lord wanted Shelley and me to be content supporting the Haitian ministry a couple in our small group had started. This included helping to raise six children in a Haitian foster home and sending several hundred

Haitian children to school each year who otherwise wouldn't have been able to go. Having done what I felt God led me to do, I felt the Lord instructing me to turn over the responsibility for the desperate child on the garbage heap—and all other Haitian children—to him. His strong shoulders can carry this enormous weight. Mine cannot.

Shelley and I, along with our small group, have continued to be open to God calling us to expand our responsibility to the poor in Haiti and elsewhere and to increase our sacrificial giving. He has done this several times. But however much responsibility God leads any of us to assume, it's crucial we leave to him what he has *not* called us to assume responsible for.

TROUBLING PASSAGES ABOUT WEALTH

As I've read books and heard speakers on the topic of wealth and poverty over the years, I've found that balance seems to be in short supply. On one hand, some rightly emphasize our need to shun greed and to care for the poor but then explicitly or implicitly rail against wealth, as though it were an intrinsic evil. This is where I was when I returned from my first trip to Haiti. On the other hand, some rightly see that God is not opposed to wealth as such but then minimize the need to shun greed and to care for the poor. In fact, many authors and speakers explicitly or implicitly promote capitalism and the accruing of personal wealth as a sign of "God's blessing." Both of these extremes are unbiblical and unhealthy.

Let me share how I gradually set aside my cynicism after my first Haiti trip.

At some point after returning to the States I became puzzled over several aspects of Jesus' ministry. For instance, why would Jesus change water into wine—for a bunch of partiers who'd already gone through all the wine the host had to offer? Why would he waste a miracle for such a trivial cause? How many disabled children in Palestine could have used that nice, superfluous display of supernatural power? After all, what's more important: helping wedding guests drink more wine than they need or helping a disabled child walk?

Then I wondered about the jar of expensive perfume Mary poured on Jesus' feet. Judas, who was in charge of Jesus' finances, objected that this perfume could have been sold and the proceeds given to the poor. Given my frame of mind at the time, this struck me as a very reasonable objection. I'd have made it myself. But Jesus *rebuked* Judas. "Leave her alone," Jesus said. "You will always have the poor among you, but you will not always have me."

Then I began to wonder why Jesus spent so much time at parties. At every turn, it seems, Jesus was eating and drinking with his disciples as well as with tax collectors, prostitutes, and every other sort of person. How many people in Palestine were not having their basic needs met while Jesus was condoning this unnecessary ingestion of food and drink?

My bewilderment hit a pitch when I came upon Paul's instruction to the rich in 1 Timothy 6. On one hand, Paul tells us to be content with what we have and not to get sucked into the pursuit of wealth. This made sense to me. But then Paul states that God, whom the wealthy are to put their trust in, is a God "who richly provides us with everything for our enjoyment." God *wants* us who are rich to *enjoy* things, I wondered? God richly provides us with everything *for our enjoyment*? From my standpoint during this time, this didn't seem right. How can God give us extra things and tell us to enjoy them when millions don't have enough to survive on?

STRIKING THE BALANCE

As I struggled to make sense of these passages, I began to understand why my guilt over every nonessential thing in my life was misguided. If the Kingdom of God is about manifesting God's will "on earth as it is in heaven," and if Jesus manifested God's Kingdom perfectly, then it must be the case that it's God's will for people to enjoy nonessential things, celebrate weddings, kick back with friends at parties, share an abundance of wine and food, and worship God extravagantly, even using expensive perfume when appropriate. So I came to see that any social situation in which people can't afford to do these things is, to this degree, less in line with God's will than one in which people can.

Jesus wasn't taking a break from the Kingdom when he celebrated nonessential things: he was just manifesting another aspect of it. We could call this the abundance aspect of the Kingdom.

Now of course, we have to balance the abundance aspect of the Kingdom with the call to live sacrificially generous lives, for we still live in a world in which 40,000 people die each day of illnesses related to malnutrition and extreme poverty. If we *only* manifest the abundance aspect of the Kingdom, we will become guilty of greed and fail to manifest the outrageous generosity of the Kingdom.

But by the same token — and here's what I needed to learn — if we *only* manifest the outrageous generosity of the Kingdom, we will fail to manifest the abundance aspect of the Kingdom and may become legalistic, self-righteous, and cynical — as I had become.

It may seem that the abundance aspect and the self-sacrificial aspect of the Kingdom are in tension with each other, but in reality they're not. The New Testament teaches us that while God loves to bless us with an abundance, the ultimate purpose for this blessing is "so that in all things at all times, having all that you need, you will abound in every good work" (2 Corinthians 9:8). And the more we give sacrificially, Paul says, the more we are given to sacrifice with. In other words, abundance and the call to sacrifice for the poor aren't at odds with one another: *they're two sides of the same coin.*

Our job, then, is never to cling to our possessions as if they belonged to us, follow God's leading in how we imitate Jesus' self-sacrificial lifestyle and care for the poor, and trust that God will use our costly sacrifices to advance his Kingdom and provide for us so we can "abound in every good work."

As we do this, we manifest the beauty of God's generous Kingdom while revolting against greed, poverty, and the Powers that fuel them.

Viva la revolution!

CHAPTER 12

THE REVOLT AGAINST THE ABUSE OF CREATION

The time has come for judging the dead ...
and for destroying those who destroy the earth.
REVELATION 11:18

It is impossible to care for each other more
or differently than we care for the earth.
WENDELL BERRY

WE'RE BURNING UP!

I am starting this chapter the day after Al Gore was awarded the Nobel Peace Prize for his fight against global warming (summarized in his Academy-Award–winning documentary, *An Inconvenient Truth*). It seems a fitting way to begin this chapter on caring for the earth and the animal kingdom.

Over the last decade, and especially over the last several years, Gore and others have warned us about the terrible things that will happen unless drastic, immediate measures are taken to curb the amount of carbon dioxide being released into the atmosphere. It is ominous, to say the least, and it's starting to have a profound impact on politics and society. More people are "going green." Even some evangelical leaders have taken up the environment cause.

I delight in this increased environmental awareness among Christians, but frankly I'm also a bit concerned. It seems to be largely motivated by the conviction that global warming is caused primarily by humans. But what if this theory turns out to be false?[1] Or what if the earth suddenly starts cooling down, like it unexpectedly did in the 1970s? Will Christians stop being environmentally conscious?

I'd like to suggest that, from a Kingdom perspective, it shouldn't make a bit of difference why the earth is warming up. Nor should it make a bit of difference if it suddenly starts cooling down. For we as Kingdom people are called to care for the earth and the animal kingdom simply because this is part of what it means to be faithful to the reign of God. Following the example of Jesus and the general teaching of Scripture, we're called to manifest God's loving care for the earth and the animal kingdom while revolting against everything that abuses creation.

THE CREATOR AND HIS PRECIOUS CREATION

Until recently, few Christians thought their faith had any implications for how they viewed the earth and the animal Kingdom. Nothing could be further from the truth.

To understand why, let's go back to the beginning.

"In the beginning," the Bible says, "God created the heavens and the earth" and he declared it all "good." Unlike many religions and philosophical schools of thought that deprecate matter as something that is inferior to spirit or even downright evil, the Bible celebrates matter as a marvelous creation of God. It is *good*.

Everything that exists is sustained, owned, and cared for by God as something inherently precious. Many passages depict God as a gardener tenderly caring for his creation. Despite the fact that everything has been tainted by the curse humans brought upon creation by our rebellion, everything still reflects God's power and loving care. Sometimes creation is depicted as a sort of worshiping congregation with every distinct thing glorifying God in its own unique way.

The Bible also depicts God as having a special love, respect, and concern for animals. Every animal was created by him, belongs to him, and is sustained and cared for by him. Just as the Lord is depicted as a gardener caring for his garden, he is also shown as a compassionate caregiver affectionately tending to the needs of his animals. "All creatures look to you," the psalmist says, "to give them their food at the proper time."

The Lord's heart is to preserve "both people and animals," and he shows compassion to every living thing he has made. For example, one of the reasons he gave to Jonah for wanting to have mercy on Nineveh was that it was home to so many animals. God clearly has a tender heart toward animals.

One of the clearest signs of the high value animals have in God's eyes is that he sometimes makes covenants with them. When God forged a new covenant with Noah after the flood, for example, he included animals. The Lord said that the placing of his bow in the sky was "the sign of the covenant I am making between me and you [Noah] and every living creature with you ..."

So too, according to Hosea, animals will be included when the Lord fulfills his promise to bring peace to the earth.

> *In that day I will make a covenant for them*
> *with the beasts of the field, the birds in the sky*
> *and the creatures that move along the ground.*
> *Bow and sword and battle*
> *I will abolish from the land,*
> *so that all may lie down in safety.*
>
> Hosea 2:18

The earth and the animal kingdom are God's handwork and are intrinsically valuable in his sight. A central job of all who submit to him is to reflect their agreement with God by how they treat the earth and care for animals.

LANDLORDS AND CAREGIVERS

The final act of creation, according to the Genesis narrative, was the creation of humans, who were created to be God's "coworkers" and corulers, carrying out his will "on earth as it is in heaven." Our original mandate was to enter into "one flesh" relationships (marry), have children, and extend God's loving dominion over the earth and the animal kingdom.

This original mandate is never retracted in Scripture. When God raised up Israel to be his vehicle for restoring the world, he commissioned them to exercise loving dominion over the land he was giving them and over the animals that inhabited it. As in many other matters, Israel was commissioned to be a microcosm of what God desired for all of humanity.

So, for example, the Israelites were told to reflect God's care for the land by giving the land a Sabbath rest every seven years. They were to allow trees to mature before they ate their fruit and were to spare fruit-bearing trees when they went to war.

Moreover, as caretakers of the land God had entrusted to them, they were continually reminded that the welfare of the land and its animals depended directly on them. If the Israelites obeyed God's decrees the land would be fruitful. If not, the land would become destitute.

As a microcosm of God's will for humanity, Israel was to extend God's compassion toward the animal Kingdom as well. For example, the Israelites were to let their farm animals enjoy the same Sabbath rest they themselves enjoyed. They were given specific instructions on how to avoid mistreating animals when they were being worked. They were to care for lost or overburdened animals, even those who belonged to their enemies. Newborn farm animals were not to be taken from their mothers too quickly. And they were to consider the produce of the land as belonging to their livestock and wild animals as well as to them.

Ultimately, when Israel and the entire world is completely brought under the reign of God, Isaiah tells us that peace will reign throughout the earth as well as the animal Kingdom. In that day,

> *The wolf will live with the lamb,*
> *the leopard will lie down with the goat,*
> *the calf and the lion and the yearling together;*
> *and a little child will lead them.*

The cow will feed with the bear,
  their young will lie down together,
  and the lion will eat straw like the ox.

Infants will play near the hole of the cobra;
  young children will put their hands into the viper's nest.

They will neither harm nor destroy
  on all my holy mountain,
for the earth will be filled with the knowledge of the LORD
  as the waters cover the sea.

Isaiah 11:6–9

THE VIOLENT, CORRUPTED CREATION

This brings us to an important but neglected aspect of the Bible's teaching about the creation and the fall. Our rebellion against God didn't only affect us. Because we were the earth's divinely appointed landlords, when we fell, everything under our authority fell as well. We brought a curse on the world and nature itself was subjected to futility. The whole creation was fundamentally altered.

For example, according to the Genesis narrative, God originally created the land to bring forth food without effort. Because of the fall, however, humans now have to toil over it "by the sweat of [our] brow" and put up with "thorns and thistles." So too, all animals were originally designed to eat "every green plant for food." Because of the curse, however, the animal kingdom is now violent and carnivorous.[2]

Not only was death not part of God's original, beautiful design for creation; according to the New Testament, it actually reflects the anti-creational activity of Satan. Christ came to "break the power of him who holds the power of death—that is, the devil." The one who has been a "murderer from the beginning" is apparently behind the death and destruction that permeates our present, fallen world. While death is a perfectly natural byproduct of the laws of nature as we find them today, the Bible suggests that it wasn't part of God's original design. Nature has to some extent been corrupted by the Powers.[3]

Jesus' healing ministry confirms this point as well since the Gospels depict all infirmities as being directly or indirectly the result of Satan's oppressive activity.[4] All these infirmities are simply "natural" byproducts of physical processes operating according to the laws of nature as we now find them. Which means, nature as we find it now has been corrupted.

THE PROBLEM OF "NATURAL" EVIL

Nature as we find it now is "red in tooth and claw," as Alfred Tennyson famously put it in his poem "In Memoriam." And as Tennyson also says, this fact poses enormous problems for those who believe the Creator is a good, peace-loving, benevolent God:

> Man ... trusted God was love indeed
> And love Creation's final law —
> Tho' Nature, red in tooth and claw
> With ravine, shriek'd against his creed.[5]

We trust that the Creator is love, but as vocal atheists such has Richard Dawkins have recently been pointing out, nature screams otherwise.[6] This is what's often called "the problem of natural evil."

While evils done by humans can be explained by appealing to free will, this explanation doesn't seem to account for evils brought about by nature. Animals rip each other apart, sometimes in prolonged, painful ways. Parasites, viruses, bacteria, diseases, and cancer kill millions and torment millions more, humans and animals alike. Earthquakes, hurricanes, tsunamis, mudslides, and volcanoes do the same. "Nature does not abhor evil," Howard Bloom notes; "she embraces it."[7]

Why would a God of love create nature to be filled with violence and suffering? According to the Bible, he *didn't*. Nature is filled with violence and suffering because it has been corrupted by

Satan and the Powers. We can of course still witness something of the power and glory of God in the beauty of nature. But we also witness the corrupting influence of Satan and the Powers.

I know this perspective is completely foreign to the contemporary Western way of understanding nature. It's even foreign to the way most Christians think about creation. Few seem to take the reality of Satan and the Powers seriously. But it's perhaps worth mentioning that it wasn't at all foreign to the early Church. The early Church fathers routinely attributed violence in nature to the work of the devil and his demons.[8] I, for one, think this remains far and away the best explanation for how nature, created by an all-good Creator, could be saturated with so much violence and pain.

Not only this, but I don't believe we can make sense of Jesus' revolt against the corruption of nature without it.

CURSING THE CURSE

There is a curious episode in which Jesus cursed a fig tree because he was hungry and it didn't have any figs. It's the only destructive miracle found in the New Testament. What's particularly puzzling is that Mark tells us the reason the tree had no figs was because it wasn't the season for figs.

On the surface, it might look as if Jesus simply lost his temper and used his supernatural power to punish a poor tree whose only crime was being in the wrong place during the wrong season. If we understand this episode against the background of the apocalyptic thought of Jesus' day, however, we see something very different going on.

Famine was widely believed to be the work of the devil in apocalyptic thought, and barren or infected fig trees became symbols of this fact. What is more, many Jews of this time believed the Messiah would free nature from Satan's grip, thus putting an end to things like famines. When we interpret Jesus' cursing of the fig tree in this light, it seems evident he was proclaiming that he was the Messiah by "cursing the curse." And in doing so, he symbolized that he was the long awaited one who would "destroy the devil's work" (1 John 3:8) and restore creation.[9]

More generally, Jesus was demonstrating that where God reigns, the demonic corruption of nature will be eventually overcome. And he was showing that, when the Kingdom is fully manifested, the cosmos will be delivered from this demonic oppression. There will then be no more famine, droughts, or hunger. Nature shall produce abundant vegetation and fruit, as it was originally designed to do.

Something similar could be said of other "natural miracles" performed by Jesus. When Jesus miraculously fed the multitudes and brought about a miraculous catch of fish, he was signifying that humans will reclaim their authority over nature when the Kingdom is fully come. When Jesus rebuked a life-threatening storm as though it were a demon, he was revealing that there are Powers wreaking havoc in creation and demonstrating that humans will have authority over these Powers when the Kingdom is fully come.[10]

So too, when Jesus raised people from the dead and was himself raised from the dead, he was revolting against the reign of death and the one who holds the power of death. And in doing this, he was pointing to a time when "the last enemy" would be utterly destroyed and death would be no more.

Jesus' ministry, we see, was a sustained revolt against the corruption of nature and the Powers that are behind it.

THE ONGOING ABUSE OF CREATION

While the mustard seed of the Kingdom has been planted, it obviously hasn't yet taken over the entire garden (Matthew 13:31–32). We continue to live in an oppressed, corrupted world. We live in tension between the "already" and the "not yet." Not only this, but we who are the appointed landlords of God's earth continue to live in rebellion against God and abuse our God-given authority over the earth. Our first mandate included taking care of the earth and animals, and I'm convinced this continues to be a foundational benchmark for how we're doing as a human race. Unfortunately, this benchmark suggests we aren't doing well at all.

For example, it's well known that the welfare of the earth's eco-system significantly depends on tropical rain forests. Yet we are currently cutting down an area of tropical forest the size of Greece *each year.* Some estimate that up to eighty percent of earth's rain forests have already been lost, the majority in the last one hundred years. A good percentage of this deforestation could be eliminated by relatively minor lifestyle changes by people in the Western hemisphere who benefit from this deforestation the most. We simply lack the will.

So too our apathy toward the environment as well as toward the suffering of the poor is largely to blame for the current clean-water crisis humanity faces. Because of pollution, irresponsible land use, hoarding, and a myriad of other factors, over a billion people on the planet have inadequate access to potable water. Preventable waterborne diseases kill approximately 10,000 children *each day.* In Africa alone, 150 children die *every hour* from illnesses attributable to the lack of clean water. All told, approximately 10 million people die *each year* because their water is unclean.

If our present computer forecasts are remotely accurate, and the earth continues to warm, this catastrophe will be magnified several times over in the coming decades. We possess the technology to significantly remedy this situation, if not correct it completely. But relief efforts have been limited because of our general reluctance to modify our water usage, lack of funding to develop wells and irrigation systems in water-deprived regions, and political and tribal conflicts in the affected regions.

We are proving ourselves to be poor landlords, and we and the earth are suffering accordingly.

Our care for animals is even more dismal than our care for the land, in my estimation. Largely due to our poor stewardship, thousands of species of animals have already become extinct or are being pushed to the brink of extinction. According to most experts, the populations of over half of all animal species are in decline. Some estimate that in the next thirty years as many as one-fifth of all species still alive today will become extinct. At our current rate of tropical forest deforestation, it's estimated that from 5 to 10 percent of all tropical forest species become extinct *every decade*.

But in my opinion, the single most telling piece of evidence that shows how poorly we're manifesting our call to care for animals is the recent creation of factory farms. Over the last century we have, to a large degree, reduced farm animals to commercialized commodities whose only value is found in how efficiently we can produce and slaughter them for profit. Consequently, more than 26 billion animals each year are forced to live in miserable, overcrowded warehouses, where there is absolutely nothing natural about their existence and where they are subjected to barbaric, painful, industrial procedures.[11] This is a far cry from what God meant when he told us to exercise "dominion."

If our care for the earth and animals is a fundamental benchmark for how we're doing as a human race, I think we can agree that we are in serious trouble.

THE KINGDOM CALL TO EXERCISE MERCIFUL DOMINION

Were this like most books on the environment and caring for animals, I would at this point express my opinion about how readers should vote, what industries they should boycott, who they should lobby, and so on. I'm not opposed to these activities, mind you. But this is a book about the Kingdom, and as in most political matters, there is simply no unqualifiedly "Kingdom" position to take on these issues. I'd actually like to pronounce my own opinions "the Christian view," but it would be arrogant and disingenuous of me to do so.

Issues surrounding what governments should do regarding the care for the earth and animals intersect with a myriad of other weighty and controversial issues that makes these matters incredibly complex and ambiguous. This is why intelligent and caring people understandably disagree about them.

Being a follower of Jesus gives us no special wisdom to resolve this complex problem. What being a follower of Jesus must do, however, is motivate us to individually and collectively *live* in a way that reflects God's original design for human dominion while revolting against everything that is incongruous with this design. Regardless of what scientific or political opinions may be in vogue, and regardless of whether the earth continues to warm or starts to cool, our call remains the same. We're to manifest God's tender care for the earth and demonstrate God's merciful love toward animals.

This means we must think critically about things like the energy we consume, the water we use and the waste we throw away. It means we must be informed about the effects our lifestyle choices—and eating choices—have on the earth and on animals.

Insofar as it is possible, we're to manifest—in the present—the harmonious relation between God, humans, animals, and the earth that will characterize the cosmos when the Kingdom is fully come. This is a fundamental aspect of what it means to be part of a Kingdom that manifests the beauty of God's original design for creation while revolting against everything that corrupts it.

Viva la revolution!

CHAPTER 13

THE REVOLT AGAINST THE ABUSE OF SEX

Flee from sexual immorality....
You are not your own; you were bought at a price.
Therefore honor God with your bodies.

1 CORINTHIANS 6:18–20

SEX AND RACQUETBALL

I once saw an episode of the sitcom *Friends* in which Monica asked a friend whom she'd begun having sex with, "Can we still be friends and have sex?"

"Sure," he replied. "It'll just be something we do together—like playing racquetball."

These days I believe the phrase is "friends with benefits." I'm told it's rather common.

This episode nicely sums up the contemporary Western view of sex. Sex is widely considered a morally neutral recreational activity, essentially no different from racquetball. Of the several hundred implicit or explicit sexualized scenes the average American views each week on television shows, commercials, or in the movies, only a fraction are between people who are in committed relationships, and less than one percent are with married couples (and most of these are to poke fun at it).

The message is not only that it's okay for sex to be enjoyed recreationally but that it's best when it's done outside of marriage. This view has so permeated America and Europe that for many—including, sadly, many Christians—the very concept of "chastity" or "sexual morality" sounds antiquated and prudish.

SEX! SEX! SEX!

The pervasiveness of the recreational view of sex is reflected in the behavior of the masses. For example, roughly 65 percent of American teens today engage in sexual intercourse before graduating from high school, while an additional 10 to 12 percent engage in oral or anal sex without intercourse. (Most young people today don't even regard these latter activities as "having sex.") By the time they get married, only about one in four women and one in five men are still virgins.

Sadly, as with all other facets of American life, statistics on the sexual behavior of professing Christians do not vary significantly from the general populace. Research suggests that being involved in an extracurricular sport does more to lower the rate of sexual activity among teenagers than does attending church. Evidence suggests that Christian abstinence programs like True Love Waits delay the average time teenagers first engage in intercourse by about eighteen months, but these programs don't generally motivate people to wait until they're married. Even more concerning, a number of studies reveal that teenagers who make abstinence pledges tend to engage in oral or anal sex *more* than others who don't, and they tend to use protection *less* when having intercourse. The undeniable fact is that young Christians have absorbed the recreational view of sex about as thoroughly as non-Christians.

Since sex has become largely severed from morality, it's hardly surprising that it's also become the culture's main tool for advertising. While advertisers have used sexuality to sell products for more than a century, the pervasiveness and explicitness of sex in advertising has taken a quantum leap since the sexual revolution of the sixties. One only has to glance through the catalogs of youth-orientated clothing stores like Abercrombie & Fitch to confirm this fact. Today's advertising could have been marketed as soft-porn only a few decades ago.

It's also not surprising that sex has become one of our culture's main tools for entertainment. Most television shows and movies (especially those orientated toward young people) now incorporate increasingly explicit sexual content, and the porn industry has virtually exploded. When I was a kid we had to sneak around to find our dads' stash. Today the kinkiest sex you can imagine is one click away.

The statistics on the use of porn in our culture are startling. Revenues from the porn industry topped 13 billion dollars in 2006, which is more than the revenue from professional football, basketball, and baseball *combined*. For the last several years, "sex" has been the single most common word fed into Internet search engines. Every second, 372 new people log onto porn sites, and it's estimated that more than half of these new users are under-aged. Whereas porn was once assumed to be a male thing, today one in three visitors to porn sites are women.

Here too, sadly, research suggests that the habits of Christians vary little from those of the general population. For example, some recent research suggests that about half of all Christian men and 20 percent of Christian women viewed porn in the last year. A survey of several Christian college campuses revealed that almost 70 percent of the male students had viewed porn within the last year. And a 2000 *Christianity Today* survey revealed that about a third of all clergy had visited porn websites within the last year.

The undeniable reality is that this recreational view of sex now permeates the Church as well as the broader culture. It would not be an overstatement to call it a crisis.

As in all things, disciples of Jesus are called to imitate him by submitting their sexuality to the reign of God. Jesus was fully human and tempted in every way that we are, yet he did not sin. Whether we are single or married, Kingdom people are called to manifest the beauty of God's original design for sexuality and revolt against the debauchery of our culture and the dehumanizing Powers that fuel it. In our sex-addicted culture, this is one of our most formidable challenges.

To be motivated to live in accordance with God's design for sexuality, I believe we need to do more than simply review the hundreds of prohibitions against sex outside of marriage found in the Bible. This is the typical approach taken by churches, and it frankly doesn't seem to be doing much good. We need to go deeper and see *why* sex is such a "big deal" to God and *why* his prohibitions are not prudish or puritanical but beautiful.

I don't believe most will be motivated to adhere to God's strong no to sex before and outside of marriage until they can fully appreciate God's even stronger yes to the beauty of sex within marriage. In what follows we'll flesh out three biblical teachings that express and explain God's strong yes to sex.

THE CREATION OF "ONE FLESH"

First, God designed sexual intercourse to create a new, sacred oneness between a man and a woman that is intended to never be broken.

At one point in his ministry the Pharisees tried to lure Jesus into a controversial debate over what constituted a permissible divorce. Moses allowed for a man to divorce his wife if he found "something indecent about her." The question was, what did "indecent" in this passage refer to? One school of thought held that virtually anything a man found displeasing in his wife could be considered "indecent." Another school taught that only something sexual in nature could be considered "indecent."

As always, Jesus refused to get entangled in this controversial quagmire. He rather appealed to God's ideal expressed in Genesis 2. He said,

> *Haven't you read ... that at the beginning the Creator "made them male and female," and said, "For this reason a man will leave his father and mother and be united to his wife, and the two will become one flesh"? So they are no longer two, but one. Therefore what God has joined together, let no one separate.* (Matthew 19:4–6)

Jesus then went on to remind the Pharisees that the only reason God permitted divorce was because of the hardness of peoples' hearts. Jesus was thus pointing out that *all* divorce involves sin, for it dissolves something God himself joined together. It destroys the "one flesh" relationship God intended for a husband and wife—a union that was supposed to last as long as their flesh survived.

Jesus' wasn't revoking the Old Testament's permission to divorce in saying this—as though people's hearts were less hard in his day than they were in Moses' day. His point was rather to expose the self-justifying motive of the questioners. Given that a new "one flesh" reality is created by God when a man and woman come together, no one can feel righteous about divorcing their wife, *regardless* of why they do so.[1]

According to Jesus, when a man and woman come together in sexual intercourse, something profound, mysterious, and spiritual is going on. God makes the *two* into a new *one*. Paul says this mysterious oneness is created *whenever* a man and woman come together, regardless of how recreational their liaison might be.

> *Do you not know that he who unites himself with a prostitute is one with her in body? For it is said, "The two will become one flesh." But whoever is united with the Lord is one with him in spirit. (1 Corinthians 6:16–17)*

Even sex with a prostitute creates a "one flesh" relationship that is supposed to never be broken! Clearly, from God's perspective sex is never merely recreational.

THE "ONE FLESH" RE-UNION

To fully grasp the depth of this "one flesh" relationship, we should pay attention to the context of the Genesis 2 passage that Jesus and Paul refer to. God had just created Eve out of Adam's side to find him a fitting helper. There's a long chauvinistic tradition of assuming "helper" (*ezer*) implies that Eve was created as Adam's subordinate, but the term actually has no such connotation. For example, Psalm 121 refers to Yahweh as our helper (*ezer*) (vv. 1–2), and I seriously doubt anyone would want to argue that Yahweh is our subordinate. The term rather has the connotation of one who brings strength.

In any event, in creating Eve, God made two persons out of one. This is why when Adam sees Eve he exclaims, "This is now bone of my bones and flesh of my flesh."

Then, most significantly, the passage immediately adds, "For this reason a man will leave his father and mother and be united to his wife, and they will become one flesh." The *reason* why a man and woman are to leave their homes and family and form a new social and spiritual reality is that their sexual complementarity is reflective of, and grounded in, an even more primordial oneness. It's appropriate for a man and woman to become one because they originally *were* one.

As God made two out of one, so now through sexual intercourse he makes one out of two. The new union is, in this sense, a *re*-union, and God is as much involved in creating the latter as he was in creating the former.

I believe this is why Paul tells husbands and wives they should no longer consider their bodies to be their own but should willingly surrender them to their spouse (1 Corinthians 7:1–5). When husbands and wives continue to consider their bodies to be their own possessions, they're simply not thinking accurately. The couple really *is* a re-united body and they should think and act accordingly.

The sanctity and beauty of the "one flesh" reality God creates is honored and protected when it's reserved for people who have pledged themselves to each other for life. But it's desecrated and destroyed when people engage in sexual intercourse outside of this sacred context.

THE SIGN OF THE HEAVENLY MARRIAGE

Second, God designed sexual intercourse to be a sacred sign of Christ's relationship with his bride, the Church.

In the course of giving instructions to husbands and wives in

Ephesians 5, the apostle Paul reminds them that all followers of Jesus are to submit to one another, regardless of social standing, gender, or ethnicity. So a husband and wife must submit to one another (v. 22). Whereas marriages under the curse tend to be characterized by power games in which each party tries to rule and control the other (Genesis 3:6), Kingdom marriages are to be characterized by doing the opposite. A marriage reflects the Kingdom insofar as husbands and wives are Christian — *Christlike* — to one another.

Paul then appeals to the analogy of Christ and the Church as he specifies what mutual submission in marriage looks like in a first-century context. In Jewish culture at that time, husbands held all the power. They were the "head" of the family. So Paul tells husbands how they are to use this culturally given power. They're not to mimic the pattern of marriage under the curse and force their will on their wives. Instead, they're to use their headship to sacrificially serve their wives, imitating the pattern of Jesus Christ. "Husbands," he says, "love your wives, just as Christ loved the church and gave himself up for her" (v. 25).

The wife is then to respond to the husband the way the Church responds to Christ. As the husband sacrificially serves her, she is to reciprocate by sacrificially serving him.

Paul then goes on to tell husbands they must love and care for their wives just as they love and care for their own bodies. And they are to do this "just as Christ does the church — for we are members of his body." Paul concludes his teaching by quoting Genesis 2:24: "For this reason a man will leave his father and mother and be united to his wife, and the two will become one flesh." And then, most remarkably, he adds, "This is a profound mystery — but I am talking about Christ and the church" (vv. 28–32).

What this teaching reveals is that the "one flesh" relationship God intends for a husband and wife is a sign of Christ's relationship to the Church. Christ has something like a "one flesh" relationship with his Church, which is his bride and therefore his body. Just as we become "one in body" with anyone we have intercourse with, so too we become "members of Christ" and are "one with him in spirit" when we submit to his reign in our life (1 Corinthians 6:16–17). The profound intimacy and shared ecstasy of sexual intercourse is a sign of the profound intimacy and shared ecstasy of the relationship God the Father intends for his Son, Jesus Christ, to have with his bride, the Church.

Yet it is vital to understand that the "one flesh" type of relationship Christ has with his bride isn't cheap. To the contrary, it's magnificently beautiful precisely because it cost Christ everything to initiate and costs us, who are his bride, everything to reciprocate. Christ lays down everything for his beloved, and we who are the beloved are to respond by laying down everything for Christ.

In the same way, the "one flesh" relationship God creates between two people only functions as a sign of Christ's relationship to the Church when it is costly. It's intended only for couples who are willing to make the ultimate sacrifice of pledging their entire lives to one another. When people enter into "one flesh" relationships without making this sacrifice, they cheapen the "one flesh" reality they've entered into and thereby violate its meaning as a sign of Christ's relationship with the Church.

THE SIGN OF THE MARRIAGE COVENANT

Third, sexual intercourse is the sacred sign and seal of the marriage covenant.

In the Bible, covenants were the means by which relationships were defined, expressed, sealed, and protected. They specified what integrity and love looked like in a given relationship. Knowing that everything humans are created to enjoy and accomplish depends on the integrity of our relationships, God takes covenants very seriously throughout the Bible. In fact, the reason animals were usually sacrificed when covenants were entered into in the Bible was to proclaim that covenant breaking leads to death.

Covenants were always sealed with a sign. The sign was something that symbolized the significance of the covenant and served as a visible reminder of the covenant. For example, when God made a new covenant with humanity after the flood, he sealed it with the sign of a rainbow symbolizing his promise to never again flood the earth. So too, when God entered into a covenant with Abraham and his descendents, he gave them the sign of circumcision. It symbolized that these people were set apart for God and that if anyone broke covenant with God they'd be cut off from the people (Genesis 17:14).

It's important to understand that the sign of a covenant was considered to be *part* of that covenant. To violate the sign was to violate the covenant. If a man wasn't circumcised, for example, he wasn't included in God's covenant with his people.

This is the role that sexual intercourse plays in a marriage covenant. It seals the covenantal vows of a couple and serves as an ongoing reminder of the "one flesh" reality they've entered into. This is why in ancient Jewish culture a couple wasn't considered married until after they'd had sexual relations. In ancient Jewish culture, as well as in many other ancient cultures, blood on the bed sheets was in some circumstances used as proof that the marriage had been sealed and proof that the bride was a virgin.[2]

In this light, whenever two people engage in sex, they are actually sealing a marriage covenant, even if that is not their intention. As we saw above, even when a man has sex with a prostitute, he becomes "one with her in body" and the "one flesh" marriage principle applies to them. This explains why if a man forced a virgin to have sex with him in ancient Israel, he *had* to marry her and could never divorce her (Deuteronomy 22:28–29). Since he already sealed the marriage covenant, the reasoning went, he had an obligation to live up to it.

While many today regard sex as a form of recreation, it's clear that in God's eyes it is anything but this. It's sobering to consider how many "one flesh" unions are being inadvertently sealed and then flippantly destroyed in our promiscuous culture and in the Church today.

HONORING THE DIAMOND

Something is precious when it is not common. It costs a great deal to purchase a diamond but costs nothing to acquire an ordinary stone, because diamonds are rare while ordinary stones are not. Sex is intended by God to be a precious and beautiful diamond precisely because it's not intended for common use. Sexual intercourse is the only place where God creates the "one flesh" reality that reflects his beautiful and costly relationship with humans in Christ. It is to be shared only by those who have paid the ultimate price of pledging their whole lives to one another.

What God knows — and what we desperately need to understand — is that our own well-being and the well-being of society depends on our treating this diamond like the rare and precious stone that it is. When we treat this diamond like a common stone — as our contemporary recreational view of sex encourages us to do — we are desecrating the "one flesh" reality it creates, disdaining its role as a sign of Christ's relationship with the Church, and violating its role as a sign and sealing of the marriage covenant. We are making a mockery of a beautiful, foundational aspect of God's plan for humans on earth. And we are, consequently, bringing destruction upon ourselves and society.

This is why God is so insistent throughout Scripture that sexual intercourse be reserved for marriage. God's not being prudish or puritanical in forbidding sex outside of marriage. He's simply trying to protect something profoundly beautiful and important. Our job as Kingdom people is to agree with him in his assessment of sex and partner with him in protecting this diamond.

In the promiscuous culture of the West, therefore, a central part of the revolution Christ has enlisted us in involves manifesting the beauty of God's original design for sexuality while revolting against the abuse of sex and the Powers that fuel it.

Viva la revolution!

CHAPTER 14

THE REVOLT
AGAINST SECULARISM

God is dead. God remains dead. And we have killed him.
How shall we, murderers of all murderers, console ourselves?

NIETZSCHE

... but we have the mind of Christ.

1 CORINTHIANS 2:16

I SUSPECT THIS FINAL CHAPTER WILL STRIKE MANY READERS AS THE MOST unusual chapter in this book. And I'm convinced that it is, in some respects, the most important. I'm certain all who take it to heart will find it the most challenging, for it requires that we revolutionize the way we Western people think, live, and experience the world moment-by-moment.

We're talking about the Kingdom call to revolt against the secular worldview.

A BRIEF BUT IMPORTANT LESSON IN HISTORY

The word *secular* comes from the Latin *saeculum*, meaning "the present world." A secular worldview, therefore, is one that focuses on the present physical world and ignores or rejects the spiritual realm or the afterlife. To the extent that one is secularized, spiritual realities like God, angels, demons, and heaven don't have a significant role in one's thought or life. Historians generally agree that the Western worldview has been growing increasingly secular since the Renaissance (thirteenth to sixteenth centuries).[1]

A number of factors contributed to the secularization of the West. The religious wars that raged between the fourteenth and seventeenth centuries played an important role, as did the success of modern science. During the Scientific Revolution (sixteenth to eighteenth centuries) scientists found that by treating the world like a closed system of causes and effects—basically like a machine—they could discover the laws by which it operates. This in turned enabled them to develop technologies that enhance the quality of human life.

The earliest scientists were Christians who saw the laws of nature as the handiwork of God, but over time God was gradually forced out of the picture. While most intellectuals during the Scientific Revolution and Enlightenment period retained some semblance of a belief in God, he was increasingly viewed as distant, uninvolved, and irrelevant. (This uninvolved view of God is often referred to as Deism.) Secularism was born.

THE AFFLICTION OF FUNCTIONAL ATHEISM

All of us raised in Western culture have been strongly conditioned by this secular worldview. Our natural orientation is toward "this present world." Of course many of us continue to believe in things like God, Jesus, angels, demons, heaven, and hell. But as every study done on the topic has shown, our beliefs tend to have little impact on our lives. The majority of Western people hold some sort of spiritual beliefs but nonetheless continue to live much of their lives as functional atheists.

Let's be honest. Most of us don't think about God in most of our waking moments. Still fewer consciously surrender to God in most of our waking moments. Even fewer experience God's presence in most of our waking moments. Our day-to-day lives are, for all intents and purposes, *God-less*.

This is the tragic affliction of secularism.

IS GOD DEAD?

This is what the nineteenth-century German philosopher Friedrich Nietzsche meant when he famously proclaimed "God is dead." He wasn't saying that God once existed and then died. He was proclaiming that the *concept* of God was functionally dead—or was at least dying. Nietzsche believed that the process of secularization had so permeated Western culture that it was no longer possible for God to be relevant in the day-to-day lives of modern, Western people.

There's no denying that Nietzsche was partly right. Secularism has indeed rendered it much more difficult for people to experience God as real and relevant. But Nietzsche was wrong to conclude that it's *impossible* for people in the secular world to rediscover the reality of God and live in this reality day-to-day. Nietzsche drew this conclusion only because he was convinced God didn't exist in the first place. So, he believed, the process of secularization was an irreversible process of humans waking up to a truer view of the world. But for people like myself who believe in God, the process of secularism isn't a process of waking up, but of falling asleep. We aren't arriving at a truer view of the world when we take God out of the picture; we're degenerating into a deceptive view of the world.

The question Kingdom people need to ask is, how can we reverse this process and wake up?

CULTIVATING AN UNBROKEN COMMUNION

As with all things about the Kingdom, the place to start is with Jesus Christ.

The Gospels tell us that Jesus never did or said anything except what he saw and heard his Father do. His life was an unbroken act of obedient surrender to his Father's will. Jesus perfectly manifested the reign of God precisely because there never was a moment in his life when he wasn't consciously surrendered to God's reign.

This is the life we're called to aspire to, and it's the absolute antithesis of a life lived according to the secular worldview. Instead of thinking, living, and experiencing reality on a moment-by-moment basis as though God does *not* exist, we're to think, live, and experience the world as though it is continually permeated with God's presence — because, as a matter of fact, *it is*. We're to live our lives with a moment-by-moment awareness of God's presence.

It's not only the example of Jesus that teaches us this. The theme runs throughout the New Testament.

For example, the need to surrender each moment to God is implied in Paul's command to take every thought captive for Christ (2 Corinthians 10:3–5). We have thoughts every waking moment of our life, so to take every thought captive requires that we surrender our thought life up to Christ moment-by-moment.

It is also implied in Paul's teaching that Jesus' disciples are to be transformed by continually renewing their minds (Romans 12:2) as well as heeding his instruction to "pray continually" (1 Thessalonians 5:17). Jesus' teaching that his disciples are to "abide" in him also entails a moment-by-moment surrender (John 15:4–10). The term *abide* (Greek *meno*) means to take up permanent residence. We aren't supposed to *visit* Jesus on occasion — during special "quiet times" or worship services (as good and necessary as these are). Instead, we're to live every moment of our life *in* Christ. We are to remain aware that we "live and move and have our being" in God.

A central task for a Kingdom disciple, therefore, is to cultivate a life of unbroken communion with God through Christ. Far from living in a "secular" world where we rarely surrender ourselves consciously to God, our goal must be to abolish the separation between the "secular" and the "holy" in order to make everything — and every moment — holy. This is our revolt against secularism.

CONFESSING CHRIST AS LORD

I'm convinced that the practice of remaining surrendered to God's presence moment-by-moment is one of the most foundational (and the most challenging) disciplines of the Kingdom. It's actually implied in the most foundational teaching of the New Testament; namely, if we confess Jesus Christ as Lord, we will be saved. To show this, I'll address two common misunderstandings of this teaching.

First, in a consumerist society like America, many treat this teaching like it was simply a good sales pitch. We can be saved—which these people think means we won't go to hell—simply by reciting this magical confession. We're basically purchasing fire insurance with a magical prayer. While submitting our life to Christ and thus having our characters and lifestyles transformed may be highly recommended, these things are not required of us to "seal this deal." We need only believe and confess.

For good consumers who are always shopping for the best deal, this offer is too good to pass up.

The trouble is—this is utter nonsense! Think about it. According to *Webster's Dictionary*, a "lord" is one who "has power and authority over others." So when a person confesses that "Jesus is Lord," they are confessing that Jesus "has power and authority" over them. And for a person to confess that someone "has power and authority" over them *means* they submit to them. So if someone confesses "Jesus is Lord" but doesn't submit to his "power and authority," they are literally contradicting themselves. Their confession is meaningless.

It's like confessing you're a married bachelor or a round square.

No wonder Jesus asked, "Why do you call me, 'Lord, Lord,' and do not do the things that I say?"

The simple truth is that when the Bible promises us that if we confess Jesus as Lord we will be saved, it's not telling us how to get cheap "fire insurance" by reciting a magical salvation formula. Rather, it's stipulating what kind of relationship we need to have with Jesus to participate in the healing and wholeness of God's reign. This relationship, by definition, must be one of submission. We are "saved" when we authentically surrender our life to Christ, enthroning him as Lord.

THE PLEDGE OF LIFE AND THE LIFE WE PLEDGE

This brings me to a second common misunderstanding of what it means to confess Jesus Christ as Lord. Though it's hardly ever discussed in contemporary Christian literature, addressing this misunderstanding takes us to the heart of Kingdom living and shows how the Kingdom is centered on a revolt against secularism.

We've seen that the profession of Christ's lordship isn't a magical formula. The confession has meaning only when it's understood to be a genuine pledge to surrender one's life to Christ. But we need to notice something that is both obvious and almost universally overlooked.

We all make an initial pledge to surrender our life to Christ, but the actual life we pledge to surrender is the life we live each moment after we make our initial pledge. For the only life we have to surrender is the life we live moment-by-moment.

Think about it. Our lives are nothing more than a series of present moments strung together. The only thing that's real is *now*. Yes, we remember the past and anticipate the future, but we do this in the present, for our life is always lived in the present. And the whole of our life is nothing over and beyond the totality of these present moments.

When we pledge our life to Christ, this is what we're pledging—to surrender each of our present moments to Christ. By definition, this can't be done all at once. It can only be done one moment at a time.

You can think of it like marriage vows. Twenty-nine years ago I looked into my wife's gorgeous eyes and pledged my life to her. But the actual life I pledged to my wife is the life I have lived each moment since I made that pledge.

The quality of my marriage, therefore, isn't decided by whether or not I made a pledge twenty-nine years ago. It's decided by how I live out that pledge *now*.

So too, the quality of our relationship with God and of our Kingdom living isn't decided by whether or not we made a pledge twenty-nine years ago or yesterday. Rather, it's determined by the extent to which we are living out that pledge *now*. Whether we're talking about marriage to another person or our marriage to Christ, our pledge is without content unless we are living it out now, in this moment—and now, in this next moment.

Unfortunately, because of the magical, consumerist view of salvation that pervades Western Christianity, we tend to assume that our life is still currently surrendered to Christ because we once-upon-a-time pledged to surrender it to Christ—which is why we tend to live largely secular lives, despite our confession of Christ as Lord. We have *theoretically* surrendered to the Kingdom, but the majority of our *actual life* is lived outside the Kingdom.

I believe that one of the most fundamental challenges Kingdom people face is to move beyond the theoretical Christianity that permeates our secularized culture, while striving to increasingly make our moment-by-moment life the domain over which God reigns. We're to seek first the Kingdom of God, Jesus said, not merely in a theoretical way that claims God is first in our life while few of our waking moments are even aware of him. We're to rather seek first the Kingdom by actually making the Kingdom the highest priority in our life—which means doing so in this moment.

And now, in *this* moment.

THE DISCIPLINE OF PRACTICING THE PRESENCE OF GOD

A seventeenth-century monk named Brother Lawrence referred to the discipline of surrendering to God moment-by-moment as "practicing the presence of God."[2] This humble monk cultivated the capacity to remain aware of God's presence, surrendering each moment to God, regardless of what else he was doing.

For Brother Lawrence, everyday chores like washing dishes became a supreme act of worship. The most insignificant details of our usually mundane lives become infused with eternal significance, he said, when we remain aware of the One "in whom we live and move and have our being." Everything that pertains to godliness, he believed, was encompassed in the call to remain aware of, and surrendered to, the presence of God each moment.[3]

If you're reading this and saying to yourself: "No way. That's impossible," I totally understand. With God's help I've been engaging in this discipline over the last decade or so, and I have to confess I'm still not very good at it. Practicing the presence of God is easy enough when I'm not doing anything else or doing things that require little attention. But when I'm immersed in conversation or a book or television or teaching—or *writing* (like now)—I find it extremely challenging.

But that doesn't matter. This is not a "Brother Lawrence God-awareness contest." The only important question is "Am I surrendered to God's presence *now*, in this moment?" Practicing the presence of God is something we strive for moment-by-moment, even if it's something we will never perfectly attain in this life.

Like me, you will undoubtedly forget to remain aware of God's presence in a few moments. But if you're open to it, before long the Holy Spirit will break through your secularized consciousness and whisper to you, "Remember me?" And when he does, our job is to yield to him and surrender ourselves to God's loving presence *in that moment*—and then seek to do so in the next moment, and then in the next.

START NOW

So if you haven't done it already—or if you started last paragraph but forgot by now—why not start this moment?

You are, right now, enveloped by God's loving presence like a molecule of water in the middle of an infinite ocean. His loving presence presses in on you like the water pressure on a submarine three miles beneath the ocean. Right now, simply become aware of this truth. Let the reality of God's loving presence be the canvass against which you experience and interpret the world around you—including reading this book.

As Brother Lawrence taught, sprinkling short spoken prayers

throughout the day will help you stay awake to God's presence. As you're reading the next couple paragraphs, for example, you might want to pause every now and then and whisper, "Thank you Lord for surrounding me with your love" or "I surrender this moment up to you." A central challenge of Kingdom discipleship is to make this sort of prayer a habit. I believe it's what Paul was getting at when he told us to "pray continually."

WAKING UP

As bad as I am at this discipline, I've learned over time that Brother Lawrence is absolutely right — the most insignificant details of our life take on eternal significance when they are integrated with an awareness of God's continual presence. In God's presence, the "secular" world disappears as it is enveloped by, and permeated with, the "holy."

As I've practiced the presence of God, there have been moments when I've suddenly become aware of the beautiful mystery of every detail of my surroundings. It's like the Kingdom breaks through my habitual, false, "secular" view of the world and explodes it from the inside out. In these moments I sense the mind-boggling miracle of existence in everything around me. A leaf twitching in the wind; a bird flying overhead; a ladybug on the blade of grass — it's all an unfathomable miracle. In these moments I am tangibly aware that all things are at every moment held in existence by "[God's] powerful word" (Hebrews 1:3). I am struck with childlike wonder. I feel like I'm looking at the world for the first time.

In moments like these I realize how much the secularized worldview has dulled my spiritual senses.

Experiences like this are magnificent, but we can't make them happen (I've tried), and we shouldn't strive for them. Our goal is not to have experiences but simply to live faithful to the pledge we made when we confessed Jesus Christ as Lord.

This is the Kingdom. It's all about our lives becoming a domain over which God reigns. And our lives are nothing more than a series of present moments strung together.

As we grow in our capacity to seek first the Kingdom of God every moment, surrendering to his love in each of the present moments that make up our lives, we increasingly manifest the beauty of God's holy Life, and we revolt against the secularism that so profoundly afflicts our world.

LISTENING TO GOD

If we live with a secular mindset, our mind is consumed with self-centered thoughts. We think about *our* plans and desires and about how things affect *us*. Our mind is a domain over which *we* reign rather than one over which God reigns.

Practicing the presence of God begins to change this. Remaining aware of God's presence and surrendering to God's will on a moment-by-moment basis draws us out of ourselves and gives us a capacity to begin to hear God's voice. Now God can begin to lead us to carry out *his* plans and wishes, rather than our own. Now we can begin to function like members of Christ's body that is actually responsive to "the head." Now we can function like sheep who hear the voice of the good shepherd. This is impossible when our mind is consumed with ourselves.

As you embark on the practice of the presence of God, I encourage you to pay attention to small promptings in your heart. This is the sort of gentle nudge we subconsciously and automatically dismiss when our mindset is secularized. I encourage you to revolt against this secularism by paying attention to these nudges.

If an action that one feels nudged to engage in is consistent with the character of Jesus Christ, I encourage you not to overanalyze it. *Just do it.* What's the worst that could happen? Even if the prompting wasn't directly from God, the worst-case scenario is that you just engaged in a loving Kingdom act. How bad is that?

A while back I drove up to a stop sign and watched a young lady with two children cross in front of me. They looked like they were rather poor, if not homeless. I whispered a little prayer of blessing on them, when suddenly I felt I was supposed to give her a hundred dollar bill I had been given earlier in the day.

So, much to the chagrin of the driver who had now pulled up behind me at this stop sign, I jumped out of my car and asked this lady: "Do you believe in God?"

She gave me a bewildered and slightly concerned look as she hesitantly responded, "Yeah."

"Good," I said as I walked toward her, "because I think he's telling me to give you this." I put the bill in her hand and said, "He loves you and is watching out for you." I quickly returned to my car and drove off. I glanced in my rearview mirror as I drove down the road and saw this young lady holding her hands over her face, crying.

Now, can I be absolutely sure this was God telling me to do this? No. I *think* it was, because I usually consider giving money to total strangers an unwise investment of God's resources. But what if I'm wrong? At worst, I'm guilty of being foolishly generous. How bad is that?

I encourage you to revolt against our culture's secularized worldview by practicing the presence of God while paying attention to the nudges in your heart. When they are consistent with the character of Christ and express love, act on them. You've got nothing to lose — except perhaps some time and money. But even these you didn't really "lose," because now they're invested in the Kingdom.

As we grow in our capacity to live under the reign of God moment-by-moment, we increasingly manifest the beauty of his ever-present love while revolting against the ugly secularism that afflicts our world.

This is the heart of the Kingdom of God.

This is the heart of the revolution we've been invited to participate in.

Viva la revolution!

WHAT can WE DO?
an ACTION GUIDE

CHAPTER 1: GIANT JESUS

Returning to the Source. For each chapter I include practical action steps that readers can take to put the chapter's teaching into practice. The first suggested action step for each chapter is a reminder to "Return to the Source." I include this in each chapter because it is foundational to everything the Kingdom is about. Everything we do in the Kingdom manifests the fullness of Life we get from God alone. He alone is to be our source of Life. We will find it impossible to live out the radical, countercultural call of the Kingdom except insofar as our core sense of worth, significance, and security is anchored in God's love for us, expressed on Calvary.

I thus encourage readers to commit to continually relinquish all idols and to return to their one true source of Life. Engaging in the classic spiritual disciplines alone and with other followers of Jesus is profoundly helpful in this regard. (For information on these, see the suggested readings at *www.gregboyd.com*.)

The spiritual discipline I and many others have found most helpful in experiencing God's fullness of Life involves the biblical and traditional practice of imaginative prayer (sometimes called "cataphatic prayer").[1] Paul teaches that while unbelievers have a veil over the minds, the Spirit removes this veil when a person submits to Jesus Christ (2 Corinthians 3:14–16). He then adds,

> *Where the Spirit of the Lord is, there is freedom. And we all, with unveiled face, beholding the glory of the Lord, are being changed into his likeness from one degree of glory to another;*

for this comes from the Lord who is the Spirit. (2 Corinthians 3:17–18, RSV)

Notice that the Spirit-inspired "beholding" Paul speaks of in this passage is one that occurs *in the mind.* "The god of this age has blinded *the minds* of unbelievers, so that they cannot *see* ... the glory of Christ, who is the image of God" (2 Corinthians 4:4, emphasis added). But the Spirit has set believers free to see "the light of the knowledge of the glory of God in the face of Jesus Christ" (4:6).

In light of this, I encourage you to regularly set aside times when you ask the Spirit to help you experience *in your mind* the glory of God in the face of Jesus Christ. Get alone in a darkened room, put on some soft lyricless background music, and imaginatively see, hear, and sense Jesus Christ expressing his perfect, unconditional love to you. Envision Jesus telling you things God's already said *about* you in Scripture, but now *experience* him expressing it to you *personally.*

You might, for example, experience the Lord looking into your eyes as he tells you he loves you with a perfect everlasting love (Jeremiah 31:3), that you are his beloved friend (John 15:5), and that nothing can separate you from his love (Romans 8:35–39). You might experience the Lord holding you as a little child, promising you that, in contrast to what some others may have done in your life, he will never leave you or forsake you (Matthew 28:20).

It's one thing to *know about* these truths, but *experiencing* the Lord communicate them to you personally is far more transforming. Experiencing the beauty of Christ's love as the source of our core worth, significance, and security sets us free to live in the Kingdom revolution.

Examine yourself. Alone and with friends, reflect on the extent to which your life mirrors the life of Christ. What difference does following Jesus make in terms of how you view others and spend your time, talents, and resources? If you were *not* a follower of Jesus, how would your life look different? Ask God to reveal to you aspects of the broader culture that you have unwittingly appropriated, especially those inconsistent with his reign.

When you discern inconsistencies, don't judge yourself harshly. Conviction is helpful, but judgment isn't. Simply remind yourself that your worth, security, and significance come from what God thinks of you as defined by Calvary. Ask God to empower you to live consistent with the Kingdom identity and to manifest his beauty. Ask fellow Jesus-followers your share life with to hold you accountable to this commitment.

CHAPTER 2: CHRIST AND CAESAR

Return to the Source. We can't hope to change the world until we ourselves are changed. When broken people—including broken Christians—try to fix the world, we only succeed in breaking it further. Our Kingdom impact can never outrun our own Kingdom transformation, and the key to personal transformation concerns where we go to get Life.

We cannot hope to advance the Kingdom as long as we get any aspect of our sense of worth, significance, or security from anything other than the King. If we get our Life from our political or national allegiances, for example, we will invariably fuse them with our (now compromised) allegiance to the Kingdom, and we will tend to view those opposed to our political or national allegiances as enemies. To keep the Kingdom holy and to live in love, we must consistently return to the one true source of Life, Jesus Christ.

Set aside regular times when you drink deeply from the infinite reservoir of God's love. Relying on the Holy Spirit, imagine Jesus expressing to you all the things Scripture says about you because of your identity in him.

Process this chapter. Alone and with friends, reflect on how this chapter impacted you. Did it challenge anything you previously thought about government, Jesus, or the Kingdom of God? How might you live differently because of what you learned? What questions does this chapter raise that you hope will be answered later in the book? Did you disagree with anything in this chapter? If so, ask yourself if yours is a legitimate counter-perspective or if it's rooted in something else.

Examine yourself. Alone and with other followers of Jesus you share life with, honestly explore what kind of power you trust. Have you allowed a "power-over" mindset to compromise your allegiance to the Kingdom of God? Are you ever tempted to think that your political opinions or activism are advancing the Kingdom of God? When you encounter conflict, as we all do, is your first impulse to *win*? Or do you try to manifest the self-sacrificial love of Christ to the person you're in conflict with? If you tend toward a power-over mindset, ask the Spirit and people you are in community with to help you discern why this is. Ask God to give you the same mindset that was in Christ Jesus when he humbled himself, set aside his divine rights, became a human, and died on the cross (Philippians 2:5–9).

Be the first fruits of the coming Kingdom. The New Testament refers to Jesus followers as the "first fruits" of a coming harvest (2 Thessalonians 2:13; James 1:18; Revelation 14:4). "First fruits" refers to fruit that ripened and was picked before the rest of the harvest and was then consecrated to God (Exodus 23:19). As the "first fruits" of God's coming harvest, our call is individually and collectively to manifest heaven *ahead of time.* Everything that will characterize the Kingdom when it's fully come should characterize us now, and everything that will be absent when the Kingdom is fully come should be absent from our life now.

In light of this, reflect on and discuss with friends what aspects of your life (thoughts, attitudes, values, behaviors, etc.) will *not* be present in heaven. When you've assessed this, remind yourself that you are called to *be* heaven on earth and that these aspects of your "old" self do not reflect who you truly are in Christ. You are empowered by the Spirit to put them off and manifest your true identity (Ephesians 4:22–32). Commit to yielding to the Spirit of Christ throughout the day, and covenant with other Kingdom people you share life with to help each another be "first fruits" of the coming Kingdom.

Wake up to spiritual warfare. How do you respond to the claim that Jesus' revolt was primarily against the Powers, not against people? If you, like most Western people, find that spiritual warfare has little or no role in your life, despite the fact that it was central to Jesus' ministry and the early church, ask God to open your eyes, as Elijah prayed for his servant (2 Kings 6:15–17). Ask God to help you see, in a spiritual way, the Powers that are behind the evils plaguing society and creation. Together with others, pray that God will help you see yourself as a soldier stationed in enemy-occupied territory whose primary task in life is to topple the enemy's empire and set humans free (2 Timothy 2:4).

CHAPTER 3: THE REVOLT AGAINST IDOLATRY

Return to the Source. We can only be free from idols to the extent that God meets our core needs. Resolve to find all your worth, significance, and security from Jesus Christ alone. Set aside special times during which you imaginatively see, hear, and sense the Lord expressing his perfect, unconditional love for you. Remind yourself daily of these truths and pray them back to God. Join with others in engaging in the classic spiritual disciplines, for they deepen your capacity to experience God in transforming ways.

Picture God. The story of Eve's succumbing to the serpent's temptation teaches us that a false, untrustworthy picture of God is at the root of our idolatry. We can't get all our Life from a God we don't trust. Everything about the Kingdom, therefore, hinges on the accuracy and beauty of our mental picture of God. Jesus came to reveal the true God. "If you see me you see the Father," he said. Honestly ask yourself, "Do I believe this?"

Here's an exercise I engage in to keep my picture of God centered on Jesus. Sit in a darkened room. Put on soft music if that helps. Then envision Jesus dying on the cross. Beneath him are vulgar guards, laughing as they cast dice for his garments. See Jesus looking down at them with loving eyes as he says, "Father, forgive them, for they do not know what they are doing" (Luke 23:34). Then see Jesus, still on the cross, looking at *you*. Hear him say something like, "[Your name], will you trust that I am the perfect expression of what God is like? Will you trust that my sacrifice reflects what *you* mean to God?" (Hebrews 1:3).

Prayerfully reflect on your thoughts and feelings as you experienced Jesus saying this. Is there a part of you that resists believing that God is *this beautiful?* Do you have competing, un-Christlike pictures of God in your mind? Identify these mental pictures and then set them aside, reminding yourself that God looks like Jesus, dying on Calvary for the people who crucified him. Exercises like this help turn mere information about Jesus (for example, that he loves all people and died for the sins of the world) into transformative truth (that he loves *me* unconditionally and died for *my* sins). As we appropriate the truth of Jesus at this deep, existential level, it truly does "set us free," as Jesus promised (John 8:32)!

Cultural idols. Reflect on and discuss with friends what you believe are the central idols in our culture? What do people crave? What do they live for? How do television shows, commercials, movies, billboards, and so on, illustrate these idols? In prayer and in dialogue with friends, explore ways you may be unwittingly influenced by these idols and what it would look like to live in revolt against them.

Take an idol inventory. Here's a way to get in touch with the idols in your life. Make a list of everything that you love and enjoy: people, possessions, abilities, personal attributes, and so on. Then go through the list and picture yourself losing that person, possession, ability, or attribute. Because you love and enjoy each thing, you would obviously experience grief if it were taken from you. This is natural. But honestly ask yourself: Would my core sense of being fully alive be diminished by this loss? If so, you may have an idolatrous relationship with that person, possession, ability, or attribute.

If you do, don't slip into self-condemnation. Rather, ask God to help you get *all* your Life from him. Picture the cross of Christ as you remind yourself that this is what your Creator thinks you're worth. Prayerfully imagine Jesus telling you, "[Your name], I give you this person [or possession, ability, or attribute] as a gift to love and enjoy. But I alone am your source of Life. All you *really* hunger for is found in me." Begin to walk in this reality.

Live with open palms. Life is our education for eternity. And one of the most important lessons God wants to teach us is how to let go of the world and cling to him. Slowly—and sometimes not so slowly—everything we cherish is being taken from us. We're all in the process of dying. Grief over these losses is as natural as it is inevitable, but to endure this process gracefully, engage in the following exercise now and then. Again make a list of everything that you love and enjoy: people, possessions, abilities, personal attributes, etc. Go through the list and imagine your hand tightly gripping each one. Then imagine the Lord lovingly and gently opening your hand. As he does this, he says, "[Your name], this is yours to enjoy—but never to *own*. Are you ready and willing to give this back to me?"

When you reach an item you have trouble releasing, ask the Lord to help you. Hear him remind you, "[Your name], I am all you really want and all you really need. Love and enjoy this thing, but don't cling to it." Ask the Lord to teach you whatever else you need to learn about your relationship with the person or thing you have trouble releasing.

Rehearse your death. Here's a prayer exercise I've benefited from for the last twenty years. Use prayer to rehearse your own death. Close your eyes and imagine you've just died (perhaps in a car crash or due to cancer). Experience what it feels like to have *everything* except the absolute core of your being taken from you. Family, friends, possessions, achievements, abilities—*everything* gone. Then imagine Jesus standing in front of you, radiant, smiling, with open arms. He welcomes you and embraces you, saying, "[Your name], I could not love you more." Try to experience the fullness of life, joy, and peace your heart craves. Then ask Jesus to help you live this way *right now.*

To experience the fullness of Kingdom Life, we have to die to everything else as a source of life. Practice dying—so that you may live.

CHAPTER 4: THE REVOLT AGAINST JUDGMENT

Return to the source. The mustard-seed Kingdom must be planted in the human heart before it can begin to branch out and take over our minds, behavior, families, neighborhoods, and the broader society. Too often people try to change the world without changing themselves. It never works (and usually makes things worse). Change must begin in our own hearts. The most fundamental question is: What is my source of Life?

It is impossible to revolt against our addiction to the Tree of the Knowledge of Good and Evil until we are getting our worth, significance, and security from Christ alone. In the midst of the busyness of our lives, we must set aside times to drink deeply from the wellspring of the beautiful love and mercy that flows from Calvary. Envision the Lord embracing you as he tells you it gave him joy to give his life for you (Hebrews 12:2) and that you are his precious work of art (Ephesians 2:10). Throughout the day remind yourself that Calvary expresses God's estimation of you and that all you really hunger for is found here. Remind yourself that Christ alone is your source of Life. Often I say to myself: "My Life is Christ, so nothing else really matters." Reinforce right priorities in your life and deepen your capacity to experience true Life by occasionally fasting from food, television, communication, or anything else as the Lord directs. Join with your friends in embarking on other spiritual disciplines and enjoying the presence of God in worship.

The blessing prayer. The first thing Jesus told his disciples to do when they came to a stranger's house was to pray a blessing on it (Luke 10:5). I believe this is still our first and most fundamental task in relation to every person we encounter. We are to express our basic agreement with God that every person we encounter was worth Jesus' dying for by blessing them—even if they curse us and mistreat us (Luke 6:27–28).

In this light, I encourage you to cultivate the habit of blessing people throughout the day. If you need to, put up Post-it notes in strategic places reminding you to do this and enter into a covenant with friends to remind one another. With every encounter during the day, simply think or quietly whisper, "Lord, I agree with you—*this* person has unsurpassable worth. Thank you for creating them and dying for them. I pray blessing on their life, in your name."

Try going to a crowded place (mall, downtown, a fair) and spend an hour or so agreeing with God that every person you see has unsurpassable worth. Pray a blessing on each one. Notice how this discipline affects your feelings and attitudes. On occasion you may experience an explosion of Kingdom Life as I did in the mall over a decade ago. Nothing releases the abundant Life of the Kingdom like hoping, believing, and praying for the best for people (see 1 Corinthians 13:6–7).

Here's another idea. Several people in the church I pastor have a ministry they call "prayer stalking." They go to crowded places, as God leads them, and adopt certain individuals to pray for. They discretely follow them at a distance, blessing them and praying for them as they feel led. It has resulted in some amazing, unintended evangelistic opportunities, though the primary purpose is simply to agree with God that each person has unsurpassable worth.

Set aside judgment. As you engage in blessing prayer, you will become more adept at noticing how many *non*-blessing thoughts you have. As you discover these, don't judge yourself. Passing judgment on yourself is no more appropriate or helpful than passing judgment on others. That's why Paul said, "I do not even judge myself" (1 Corinthians 4:3). Instead, simply remind yourself that God alone is judge and that your only job as a Kingdom person is to agree with him that every person you see has unsurpassable worth.

Love enemies. Think of the person it is hardest for you to love. Perhaps they have harmed you or continue to harm you or other people in some way. Now, it's okay if your *feelings* about this individual don't change right away, for Kingdom love is not about feelings. It's about agreeing with God's assessment of people's worth. So ask God to help you love this person as God loves you. Remind yourself that Jesus died for *you* when you were *his* enemy, and ask him to empower you to have this attitude toward your enemy (Ephesians 5:1–2). Then, as you envision this person in your mind, express your agreement with God that this individual has unsurpassable worth by praying a blessing prayer for that person. Finally, ask God to give you his wisdom about how you can express this person's unsurpassable worth to them in more concrete ways.

Note that loving a person as Christ loves you *doesn't* necessarily mean that you trust them, want to be their friend, or even want to be around them. I may wisely mistrust my neighbor or even a relative to babysit my grandson, for example, but I'm still commanded to love that person. You may discern that it's unhealthy for you to be in relationship with a certain dysfunctional or malicious person, but you're still commanded to love them.

CHAPTER 5: THE REVOLT AGAINST RELIGION

Return to the Source. Like everything else about the Kingdom revolution, if we're going to manifest the scandalous grace of God and revolt against religion, we must begin with ourselves. The task for each one of us is simply to *be* the Kingdom. We can't hope to help others get free from religion and manifest the beauty of God's indiscriminate, relentless agape-love unless we are being transformed by God's scandalous grace and freed from religion ourselves. So long as our hearts are hungry, we can *exchange* our idols but can never be truly *free* from them.

The only way to get free from religion is to continually get Life from the one non-idolatrous source of Life there is—Jesus Christ—and resolve in our minds that *all* of our worth, significance, and security comes from what God thinks of us, as demonstrated on Calvary.

We can only love others as Christ loves us if we regularly experience Christ loving us. It's imperative, therefore, that Kingdom people take time to allow the Spirit to open their hearts and minds to the beauty of Christ's love for them, for as we behold this beauty we are transformed *into* this beauty (2 Corinthians 3:17–18). Imaginatively see, hear, and sense the Lord reminding you that you were bought with an infinite price and thus have unsurpassable worth (Mark 10:45; 1 Corinthians 6:20; 7:23). Experience the Lord tenderly assuring you that you are completely forgiven and have been given the righteousness that comes from him (Romans 5:1; 1 Corinthians 6:20; Ephesians 1:7; Colossians 1:14). Envision the Lord interacting with you like this throughout the day, as you offer up words of praise and gratitude in response. Engage in the spiritual disciplines with those you share life with and spend quality time together worshiping and basking in the presence of God.

Get free from theological idolatry. Ask yourself, "If I were proven wrong about all my beliefs—except my core belief that God's attitude toward me is revealed in Jesus Christ—would my sense of worth be lessened?" If the answer is yes, it's an indication you are using your beliefs as a source of Life. It's okay to regard beliefs as important. They are. But Christ *alone* is our source of Life. If your identity is wrapped up in the rightness of your theology, I encourage you to spend more time experiencing God's perfect and unlimited love for you—a love that is unwavering even if every theological opinion you have turns out to be wrong.[2]

Unmask religion. Prayerfully reflect on your life and that of your community of Jesus followers. Do you individually and collectively attract or repel those most judged by society and religion as "sinful"? If the honest answer is that you tend to repel them, ask yourself why this is so. Is religious idolatry suppressing the unconditional love of the Kingdom in your life or the life of your faith community? Discuss with your community of Jesus followers how you can start communicating God's love to those most judged by society and religion. How can you start befriending and "washing the feet" of gays, transvestites, drug addicts, prisoners, and others who have traditionally been judged harshly and rejected by Christians?

Wake up to religious judgment. Alone and with friends, prayerfully reflect on and discuss the following question: Are there certain types of sinners you habitually feel superior to? Are there certain types of sins in other people's lives that you feel you're condoning if you don't show your disapproval of them? For example, it has been my experience that many evangelicals feel they are condoning gays if they don't express their disapproval of them. Ask yourself, would you feel this way if these people were guilty of *other* types of sin—if, say, they didn't share their wealth with the poor (greed); if they talked negatively about others behind their backs (gossip); or if they ate more than they needed (gluttony)? If you find that you tend to judge some sins more harshly than others, ask yourself why this is. If you're ruthlessly honest, you're likely to discern that it's because you've been conditioned by religion to condemn some sins (such as homosexuality) more harshly than others (such as greed, gossip, and gluttony). Let this serve as a sign that you are still in bondage to religion and need to drink more deeply from the bottomless well of God's love. Repent (turn) from your judgment and ask God to give you the humility that genuinely sees your own sin, whatever it may be, as a plank while viewing other people's sin, whatever it may be, as a mere dust particle (Matthew 7:1–3).

Wash feet. Get a mental image of Jesus washing the dirty, smelly feet of his disciples, knowing they will deny him hours later (John 13:1–5). Since you are called to imitate Jesus in this activity (John 13:14), imagine yourself washing the feet of the people you tend to judge as being the worst of sinners. As you do this, hear Jesus say to you, "As I have loved and served you—and not judged you—so you are to love and serve others and not judge them."

Did any part of you have trouble with this picture? If so, it may indicate a stronghold of judgment in your life. Bring that thought captive to Christ by reminding yourself that your sin is worse than any sin you may see in others. If your common sense screams that this is ludicrous—such as, "No way is my greed as bad as that person's homosexuality!"—remind yourself that you're called to live in obedience to Jesus, not to the "common sense" of your religious or cultural conditioning. Remind yourself that your main job in life is to *imitate* Jesus. Pray and discuss with friends how, together, you can concretely "wash the feet" and express God's humble, servant love toward those you are tempted to think are worse sinners than yourself.

CHAPTER 6: THE REVOLT AGAINST INDIVIDUALISM

Return to the Source. It may seem ironic, but it is impossible to enter into relationships that reflect the love of the triune community unless we ourselves are getting our Life from God. We all need deep, meaningful relationships, but they are not to be our source of Life. When our need for worth, significance, and security isn't met by our relationship with God, we end up using people to try to meet this need. Kingdom relationships shouldn't be a means by which we *get* Life from others. Rather, relationships are meant to express and share in the fullness of Life we receive from God. Not only this, but as long as we're living life in a hungry mode, we will find it impossible to resist the continual pull of our consumer culture. We unwittingly buy the lie that our worth, significance, and security are rooted in what we can acquire, possess, and achieve. This in turn motivates us to make striving for things a higher priority than cultivating deep, but often time-demanding, relationships. So long as we're hungry for Life, we will lack the motivation and capacity to participate in genuine Kingdom communities.

I encourage you, again, to continually return to the one true source of Life. Make time to rest in the unconditional love of God, envisioning him holding you, healing you, and rejoicing over you. Individually and with others, engage in spiritual disciplines that deepen your capacity to empty yourself of worldly clutter and make more room for God's presence.

Introspect. Prayerfully reflect on the extent to which you have been conditioned by Western individualism and consumerism. Are you in authentic "Kingdom relationships"? Have you committed to loving and serving a community of people? Are there people in your life who know you well enough to notice when things are wrong and who care enough to address it? Are there disciples of Jesus whom you trust enough to give permission to point out aspects of your life that are possibly not consistent with your commitment to the Kingdom? Are their friends with whom you're willing to submit significant life decisions for discernment? Do you have a community of people who share your Kingdom vision and with whom you minister to carry out this vision?

If the answer to these questions is no, prayerfully consider why. Is it because having relationships is not a high priority for you? Is it because you fear relationships like this would impinge on your personal freedom? If so, ask the Lord to help you embrace a more Kingdom set of priorities and become freed from the stronghold of Western individualism.

Revolt against the consumer system. As a westerner, you live in a consumer culture that systematically conditions you to consume more and more. You are bombarded with advertisements trying to convince you that your life isn't full unless you have what they're selling. Not surprisingly, the two main things Americans do with their leisure time is watch television and shop. The first brainwashes us to do the second, and the second requires that we work incessantly to pay for all our stuff we're brainwashed to buy. Consequently, most Americans have neither the time nor the inclination to cultivate meaningful relationships. The Powers have reduced us to mice on a treadmill futilely chasing the cheese of the American dream.

Revolt against the Powers! A great place to start sensitizing yourself to this consumerist treadmill is by viewing a short video called *The Story of Stuff* (available at *storyofstuff.com*). Notice how many advertisements bombard you each day. Get in the habit of letting them serve as reminders to get *all* your Life from Christ. Commit to simplifying your life and carving out time for meaningful relationships (as well as ministry and relaxation and other necessary things our consumer culture steals from us). Watch less television and spend the extra time with family, friends, and those God calls you to minister with and to.

Enter into community. If you're not in a committed small group, join one. If your church doesn't have a small-group ministry, use whatever influence you have to start one. In the meantime, I encourage you not to wait for your church to get its act together but prayerfully seek out other Jesus followers with whom you can forge Kingdom relationships, engage in Kingdom worship, and carry out Kingdom ministry. You might start by simply inviting other Christians over to discuss books that teach on the importance of small groups (or "house churches") and that give advice on how to go about growing them. (For suggested readings, see *www.gregboyd.org.*)

If you already belong to a committed small group, consider ways you can bring more of the Kingdom into your fellowship. Talk about ways you can build more trust with one another so you can give each other permission to speak into each other's lives. Discuss ways you can minister together, worship together, and share more of life with one another. Read up on and discuss how you can transition from being merely a group of friends to a New Testament *church*. (For suggested readings, see *www.gregboyd.org.*)

CHAPTER 7: THE REVOLT AGAINST NATIONALISM

Return to the Source. We cannot hope to revolt against the idol of nationalism as long as any element of our identity, worth, significance, or security is rooted in our national allegiance. We can pledge our total allegiance to Christ alone only if we're getting all our Life from him. So I encourage you to return regularly to the one true source of Life. In special times of prayer, vividly imagine Jesus lavishing his love on you. Envision him telling you he has reconciled you to God, made you a citizen of heaven, and commissioned you to be his coworker and ambassador of the Kingdom (1 Corinthians 3:9; 2 Corinthians 5:17–20; Philippians 3:20). Throughout the day, remain aware of God's loving presence, reminding yourself of these truths and giving praise to God that all you really need and long for is found in Christ. Together with your community of Jesus-followers, make time to worship God and engage in spiritual disciplines as you help one another experience God's Life more profoundly and get increasingly free from nationalism and all other forms of idolatry.

What does your nationality mean? Alone and with friends, reflect on what it means for you to be American, German, British, or whatever nationality you identify with. There's nothing wrong with feeling good about your nationality, but ask yourself honestly if any element of your identity, worth, significance, and security is rooted in this nationalistic identity.

To help do this, write out a list of values you embrace because of your nationality. For most Americans, that would include the right to life, liberty, and the pursuit of happiness. With the help of your community, honestly assess how you would be impacted if any of these values were threatened? Would your sense of worth, significance, identity, or security be fundamentally altered? If so, this is an indication that you are not yet getting all your Life form Christ. Commit to seeking first the Kingdom of God and getting all your Life from Christ alone.

Assess your life. Reflect on and discuss the extent to which the Church in your nation reflects the values of your nation—in contrast to the values of the Kingdom. Is the church known for how it resists the ideologies and values of the nation or for the way it embraces and defends them? Apply these questions to your own church, small group, and life.

If aspects of your life, small group, or church reflect idolatrous nationalism, ask God and discuss with friends what can be done to get free from their bondage and to become singularly devoted to the Kingdom revolution.

Pledge allegiance? Discuss with friends whether it is appropriate for Kingdom people to pledge allegiance to their country and its flag? If you participate in this nationalistic ritual, what does it mean to you and how does it relate to your pledge of allegiance to Christ and the Kingdom he came to establish?

Become a transnational Christian. As citizens of the Kingdom of God and ambassadors of Jesus Christ, it is crucial that we resist the pull of the Powers that want us to adopt a myopic, tribal, nationalistic outlook. We must never allow our love and concern for others to be conditioned by what nation and culture they happened to be born into. While our fallen hearts and minds tend to care about "our nation" and "our people" more than others, the Kingdom heart and mind must love and care *indiscriminately*, as Jesus commanded (Matthew 5:43–48). But given the oppression of the Powers, this takes discipline. Here are a few suggestions to help your outlook to remain global:

* Be intentional about stretching your tastes and preferences by regularly eating food and experiencing entertainment from other countries. Go out of your way to cultivate relationships with people whose nationality is different from your own. Learn their culture, customs, and beliefs.

* Pay attention to major events around the world and join with others in regularly praying for people adversely affected by them. As you do so, ask God to help you empathize with these people. Try to imagine, as vividly as you can, what they might be going through. Be open to God leading you and your Kingdom community to sacrificing some of your own resources to assist those who are suffering.

* Along with the community of disciples you share life with, pray about adopting a country or region to pray for and perhaps minister to. Learn about the history, culture, beliefs, and customs of this nation or region. Pray about the possibility of supporting indigenous ministries in this area. Consider going to this area on a short-term mission trip.

* Consider opening your home to foreign-exchange students.

* This one is especially challenging for many Americans, but I encourage American Kingdom people to make an earnest attempt to understand why various groups around the world do

not appreciate—if not disdain—America. I'm not suggesting Kingdom people need to agree with these anti-American views. But the very attempt to understand the views of "an enemy" helps us rise above a simplistic "good versus evil" dichotomy that nationalism tends to afflict people with. An interesting (and highly controversial) book to begin one's study is Ziauddin Sardar and Marryl Davies, *Why Do People Hate America?* (Cambridge, UK: Icon Books, 2003).

CHAPTER 8: THE REVOLT AGAINST VIOLENCE

Return to the Source. Getting free from violence in thought, word, and deed is impossible as long as we try to acquire Life from any source other than Christ. Paul teaches us that life in the "sinful nature" is inevitably characterized by hostile attitudes and behavior (envy, hatred, fits of rage, discord, and factions; see Galatians 5:20–21). Such a "sinful nature" is an inevitable outworking of idolatry, for to the extent that we cling to anything other than God as our source of identity, worth, significance, and security, we are sucked into the conflict-filled idolatrous feeding frenzy of the oppressed world (see chapter 3). Our idols are perpetually threatened, and we cannot help feeling hostile toward anything or anyone that threatens our source of Life.

The key to getting free from our own tendency toward violence, therefore, is to die to the idolatrous way of living and commit to getting all our Life from the one true source of Life, Jesus Christ. Only when we can say with Paul, "I no longer live, but Christ lives in me," can we be free of the impulse to defend our life and all we hold dear with violence (Galatians 2:20; cf. Romans 6:6). As we learn how to die to ourselves and yield to the Spirit of Christ within us, we become filled with the full measure of God's love (Ephesians 3:19) and begin to manifest "the fruit of the Spirit" instead of the "sinful nature." Our thoughts, words, and deeds become increasingly characterized by "love, joy, peace, patience, kindness, goodness, faithfulness, gentleness and self-control" (Galatians 5:22).

I encourage you, therefore, to regularly spend time alone with Christ, experiencing him ascribing unsurpassable worth to you and setting you free from the need to cling to idols, including the idol of biological life itself. I encourage you to cultivate a Life-giving relationship with Christ throughout the day. Train your mind to remember that you have died to the world but are alive in Christ (Colossians 3:3). I frequently affirm the statement, "Life is Christ, nothing else really matters." (This is especially helpful in stressful situations.) Remind yourself throughout the day that you are always to abide in God's loving presence and that all your identity, worth, significance, and security come from him alone. Everything you *really* need is found in him.

Commit to nonviolence. Violence seems so natural in our fallen, oppressed state that few of us will make progress in getting free from it unless we make a covenant with God and others to purge it from our lives. I encourage you to ask God's forgiveness for any past violence in your life. Make a commitment to God and those you share life with to live a life free of violence. Encourage those in your Kingdom community to study this subject together (for suggested readings, see *www.gregboyd.org*) and to join you in making this commitment.

This commitment doesn't necessarily mean you will actually be able to refrain from violence in certain circumstances—for example, if a loved one were attacked. I myself *hope* I'd respond nonviolently, but I can't be certain. A commitment to nonviolence means you're pledging to walk in that *direction*, practicing peace day-by-day. The more we develop a Christlike character, the more likely we are to respond to a hostile enemy in a Christlike way if they were to attack us or a loved one.

Cleanse the heart. Our violent tendencies will never stop unless idol-rooted violence is purged from our hearts. Ask God and others in your small group to help you examine yourself to locate any hostility you harbor toward others. As mentioned in chapter 4, one of the best ways to flesh out non-Kingdom sentiments hidden within us is to practice agreeing with God about people's unsurpassable worth by blessing everyone you happen to come upon or think about. Be particularly intentional to bless people whose behavior you *don't* approve of.

As you bless them, be attentive to any thoughts and attitudes that *disagree* with your blessing-stance toward people. When you identify non-Kingdom thoughts and attitudes, do not pass judgment on yourself. Simply turn from them (repent) and embrace thoughts and attitudes that agree with the estimation God expressed toward these people on Calvary. Then ask God and your small group to help you discern *why* you harbor hostile thoughts and attitudes. Behind every anti-Kingdom thought and attitude (as well as action) lies a false source of Life. So ask God as well as your Kingdom community to help you locate the idol in your life that is producing this "work of the flesh."

Do good to enemies. Jesus and the New Testament teach that we are not only to refrain from violence toward enemies, we are to do *good* to them. In light of this, prayerfully consider ways you and your community can do good to people you identify as "enemies."

For national enemies like Osama Bin Laden, it's likely the only good you can do is to pray for them, something Jesus specifically commands (Luke 6:27–28). While millions are praying curses upon such enemies, I encourage you and your Kingdom community to pray Jesus' prayer of forgiveness for them (Luke 23:34). Pray for a change in their heart and that they might learn the joy of walking in peace rather than hatred or violence. Praying for a life transformation in someone like Bin Laden may seem naïve, but we are called to live in love, and love perseveres in hope for everyone (1 Corinthians 13:7).

We must pray for our personal enemies as well—neighbors, coworkers, relatives—all who may have something against us. In these cases though, there are probably more concrete ways we can serve them. Consider ways in which you might be able to sacrifice of your time, energy, and resources to bless or help them. As you do so, look for opportunities for reconciliation. The ultimate victory of good over evil occurs when an enemy becomes a friend.

Become a peacemaker. Jesus calls his disciples to be "peace makers" (Matthew 5:9). One primary way to do this is by using the unique authority we have to affect the world through prayer to influence leaders in a peaceful direction. Prayer is also a main tool Kingdom people are to use to bring Kingdom peace into conflicted situations in all our personal relationships as well as in our communities. As Walter Wink argues, prayer confronts the Powers that fuel hostility and is therefore a form of "social action."[3]

Kingdom people are called to be peacemakers in every other possible way as well. Wherever there is hostility between people with whom we have some influence, we are to seek God's wisdom about how he might use us to bring about reconciliation (James 1:5; 3:13–17). In our personal relationships and in our communities, we are to be people who always look for ways to bring peace where there is hostility.

Along the same lines, we who live in democratic societies are allowed some influence in our government by voting and participating in the political process in other ways. If you choose to participate in this process, prayerfully reflect on how you can best influence leaders and support policies that will further the cause of peace. Of course, as we noted in chapter 2, we must always remember that governments remain under the strong influence of Satan. We must also always respect the inherent limitations and ambiguity of political "solutions" as well as their inherent "power over" methodology. In this light, we must never confuse our particular way of influencing politics with our distinct Kingdom call by labeling our political views "Christian."

What *is* a distinct Kingdom approach to global conflict is to not only pray for peace in conflicted regions, but to actually *go* there to work for peace. Not everyone is called to this form of peacemaking, of course, but some are. A number of organizations train and equip groups of Kingdom people for the difficult and dangerous task of entering conflict situations to help warring factions sit down together and work toward peaceful resolutions. I encourage readers to be open to the possibility that God would lead them to join one of these groups, whether as a short-term or lifelong worker.

One such organization is Christian Peacemaking Teams (*cpt.org*). Since 1984, CPT has sent peacemakers to conflicted areas such as Gaza, Haiti, Bosnia, Palestine, and Iraq. Their motto is to "get in the way" of the violence in order to bear witness to an alternative, nonviolent way of dealing with conflict. You may recall that in 2005 four CPT workers were taken hostage in Iraq, and one (Tom Fox) was murdered. This kind of work is certainly not for the fearful.

Other organizations that train people for similar peacemaking ministries are Witness for Peace (*witnessforpeace.org*), Peace Brigades (*peacebrigades.org*), and Nonviolent Peace Force (*nonviolentpeaceforce.org*, though this latter group is not specifically Christian).

There are currently several thousand courageous souls who participate in these global peacemaking ministries. But one wonders what would happen if there were several *hundred* thousand such workers? What would happen if there were as many soldiers laying down their lives to fight for peace on behalf of the Kingdom of God as there are soldiers fighting violently on behalf of their particular version of the kingdom of the world? While it would certainly cost many Kingdom people their lives, I believe it would cost far less lives than the violent approach has proven to cost throughout history.

Even if the peacemaking approach to conflict were not demonstrably successful in any particular conflict, it would still bear witness to the reality of the Kingdom that is "not from this world." By revolting against the ugliness of violence, it would manifest the beauty of the Jesus-way of living. And this is the one goal that must define the very being of all followers of Jesus Christ.

CHAPTER 9: THE REVOLT AGAINST SOCIAL OPPRESSION

Return to the Source. We *class*-ify people because we're socially conditioned to do so. And we're socially conditioned because, on some level, it's how those who benefit from these class divisions try to find Life. We will find it impossible to revolt against the Powers behind classism unless we are getting our worth, significance, and security from Christ alone.

As in all matters pertaining to the Kingdom, it is vital that we return to the one true source of Life. In special times of prayer and throughout the day, drink deeply from the bottomless well of God's love for you. Together with other Kingdom people you share life with, spend time in worship and engage in the spiritual disciplines to help one another grow in your capacity to experience and be transformed by God's perfect, unwavering, unconditional love.

Process this chapter. Alone and with friends, prayerfully reflect on how this chapter impacted you. Did any of it make you feel hopeful and excited? Were there parts that surprised or offended you? Did this chapter challenge any assumptions you've had about social classes and the call of the Kingdom to abolish them? Together with your small group, reflect on the extent to which your view of people is polluted by your social conditioning to class-ify people.

Live out the Jubilee Kingdom. Talk to God and your Kingdom community about how you can live free from class judgment and manifest the classless Jubilee Kingdom. Here are some suggestions:

- Pray regularly for those oppressed by society's way of classifying them.
- Read and discuss with your small group books on the role class plays in America and in the Church. (For suggested readings, see *www.gregboyd.org.*)
- As you cultivate the practice of blessing others, pay special attention to those whom society tends to ignore—the average-looking woman trying to haul a suitcase up some stairs, for example. Following Jesus' example, when you see a need, *act* on it. You'll discover opportunities to serve "the least of these" all around you.
- Jesus said that when you host a feast, invite "the poor, the crippled, the lame, the blind" (Luke 14:12–13). These were the beggars, misfits, and outcasts of first-century Jewish culture. Think about hosting a party and inviting people our society

(and likely the church) tends to deem lower class, misfits, and outcasts—people who may not have been invited to anyone's party for a long time. More broadly, discuss with your Kingdom community ways you can invite "outcasts" into your lives by developing meaningful relationships with them.

- If you live in a homogenous suburb, honestly reflect on why you do so and discuss this with your Kingdom community. Has God placed you there for Kingdom service? Or, perhaps influenced by a typical American mindset, do you live there simply because you prefer it and can afford it? If you suspect the latter, seek God's will for a clear Kingdom vision on where and how you're supposed to live.
- If you are called to live in a homogenous suburb, consider ways you can alter your lifestyle to encounter and befriend people who are not "in your class." Make adjustments in where you shop, go for coffee, get your car fixed, go for entertainment, and so on. Doing this will help you experience a life enriched by freedom from class myopia.
- Continually submit your time, money, and resources to the Lord as well as your small group to discern whether the amount you spend to support your lifestyle versus the amount you invest in the Kingdom is in accordance with his will.
- Engage in ministries that cross class lines. Together with friends, visit and befriend elderly people. Join a prison ministry. Participate in inner-city youth ministries. Volunteer in soup kitchens or homeless shelters. Commit to volunteering at an inner-city church.
- If you are able to, go on regular short-term mission trips to serve impoverished neighborhoods or countries.

Help your church become a Jubilee Tribe. Talk to God and others about what your church can do to more faithfully and consistently revolt against the classism of your culture and the Powers that fuel it. Here are some suggestions:

- Once you've studied the role that class plays in America and the Church, and have embarked on the journey of living free from classism, offer to lead a book study or film-centered discussion on the issue. (A good film to launch a discussion with is *People Like Us*. For suggested readings, see *www.gregboyd .org*.)

• If your church is not currently embracing and utilizing people with disabilities, help start a ministry that both encourages and disciples people with disabilities and provides opportunities for them to use their gifts. For assistance and resources, see *faithaliveresources.org*, *friendship.org*, and *joniandfriends .org*.

• If your church is not currently engaged in a prison ministry, help start one or encourage the leadership to partner with other churches that already are. For help, check out Chuck Colson's Prison Fellowship at *prisonfellowship.org*.

• If you're in a suburban church, encourage your leadership to enter into mutually beneficial relationships with churches that represent a different socioeconomic level. If you're in a suburban church and already regularly volunteer at an inner-city church, offer to make this opportunity available to others in your congregation.

• If your church has no ministry to the elderly, start one. For help in ministering to people in nursing homes, check out *faithfulfriends.org/manuel.html*.

• If your church does not allow women to minister in certain areas where they may be gifted (such as preaching, teaching, or pastoring), encourage the leadership of your church to re-open this issue by carefully studying the matter. (See *www. gregboyd.org*.) If the leadership of your church is dogmatically opposed to this, I encourage you to prayerfully consider with your small group whether in fact this is the larger church body God is calling you to align with. (Think about it. Would you align yourself with a church body that, say, continued to condone slavery as it was practiced in the first century or that forbade a person to exercise their spiritual gifts on the basis of their race?)

CHAPTER 10: THE REVOLT AGAINST RACISM

Return to the Source. Like everything else the Kingdom revolts against, racism is a form of idolatry. We cannot hope to revolt against it and manifest the "one new humanity" unless we are getting our Life from a source greater than our race. While it is healthy to feel good about our ethnicity and culture, as a Kingdom people, our identity, worth, significance, and security must come only from what God thinks about us, as evidenced on Calvary.

Set aside special times to allow the Spirit to bring you into a vivid, concrete, imaginative encounter with the living Lord. See him, hear him, and sense him lavishing his unsurpassable love, joy, and peace on you. Experience him telling you he's made you his own child and that his own joy is made complete in you (John 1:12; 15:11). Envision him delighting over you as he reminds you he's given you an eternal and infinitely rich inheritance and is conforming you to his likeness (Zephaniah 3:17; Ephesians 1:11, 18). Throughout each day remind yourself of these truths and give thanks that your identity is found in Christ and nothing else. Have regular times of worshiping with the small group of disciples you share life with in which, together, you experience the abundant Life that flows from God.

Process this chapter. Reflect on and discuss with friends what impacted you most in this chapter. Were there sections that made you feel hopeful and excited? Were there sections that made you feel angry, guilty, offended, scared, confused, or hopeless? Did this chapter challenge assumptions you've had about race or about racial reconciliation?

Cultivate cross-cultural relationships. If you do not have meaningful relationships with people whose ethnicity is different from your own, talk to God and your friends about what you can do to begin to cultivate such relationships. Here are a few suggestions:

* Go out of your way to cultivate friendships with people in your neighborhood who are ethnically different from yourself.

- If you live in a homogenous neighborhood, go to more diverse neighborhoods to shop, get coffee, have your hair cut, get your car fixed, and so on.
- If you're white and live in a mostly white suburb, prayerfully reflect on whether you live there because it suits your personal preference or whether you believe God *wants* you to live there. (I'm not trying to hint that living in white suburbs is against God's will. I'm simply suggesting we all need to seek God's will on where and how we live.)

Revolt against racism. Prayerfully dialogue with those you fellowship with about what you can do together to revolt against racism and better manifest the "one new humanity" of the Kingdom. Here are some suggestions for you and your small group to consider:

- Pray for people who are oppressed by racism in America and around the globe.
- Educate yourself. Read up on the realities of ongoing racism. (For suggested readings, see *www.gregboyd.org*.) Participate in seminars and workshops on racial reconciliation.
- Volunteer at a church whose ethnic and racial makeup is significantly different from your own.
- If you're in a position to do so, consider serving as a foster parent for children whose ethnicity is different from your own.
- Volunteer and/or contribute to a ministry dedicated to racial justice, ethnic diversity, and reconciliation.
- Learn about other cultures in your area. Go out of your way to learn about other cultures' distinct food, music, and arts by frequenting their restaurants, art shows, and concerts. Continually revolt against our fallen tribal tendency to live monoculturally.
- If you're in a position to do so, host foreign-exchange students in your home or invite some over for a holiday dinner.
- If you're white and choose to participate in the political process, speak to people of other ethnicities about the concerns

that weigh on their hearts and what they think should be done about them.

Help your church manifest the "one new humanity." Talk to God and others about what your church can do to better revolt against racism and manifest the "one new humanity" created in Christ. Here are some suggestions:

- If your church does not emphasize racial reconciliation the way it emphasizes other aspects of what Jesus lived and died for, encourage the leadership to begin studying the issue.
- Encourage the leadership to consider hiring a racial-reconciliation consultant. The congregation I pastor was greatly helped by the relationships we developed with the wonderful people at Salter McNeil and Associates (*saltermcneil.com*).
- Offer to lead a book study and discussion group on the topic of racial reconciliation at your church or offer to sponsor a racial-reconciliation film viewing and discussion group. (A great one to start with is *The Color of Fear*, put out by Stir Fry Productions.)
- Encourage the leadership of your church to prayerfully consider moving toward more ethnically diverse forms of worship. If there are people from different ethnic groups in the neighborhood of your church, encourage your leaders to take particular care to incorporate their cultural music into some of your worship.
- If there are people from different ethnic groups in your church's neighborhood, ask them how your church could welcome and serve them. If there are some for whom English is a second language, encourage the leadership to consider making signs inside and outside your church bilingual. If the need is present in your community, consider helping your church develop an ESL (English as a Second Language) program.
- Encourage the leadership of your church to enter into mutually beneficial relationships with churches whose ethnic makeup is different from your own. If you have been regularly volunteering at a church that is racially different from

your own, offer to help make this opportunity available to others in the congregation.

- Finally, if the leadership of your congregation refuses to move forward on these issues, prayerfully consider the possibility that God would lead you to join a congregation that *is* passionate about them. (Think about it. Would you attend a church that refused to preach that Jesus died for the forgiveness of our sins? Jesus died to reconcile the races within his Kingdom community as well.)

CHAPTER 11: THE REVOLT AGAINST POVERTY AND GREED

Return to the Source. We hoard resources when we view them as a source of Life. We cannot manifest the beauty of God's outrageous generosity and revolt against greed as long as we're entrapped by this idolatry. So again, return to the true source of Life and get your worth, significance, and security from what God thinks about you, as evidenced by Calvary. Set aside times in which you bask in God's love for you. Imaginatively see, hear, and sense Jesus reminding you that you are filled with all the fullness of God (Ephesians 3:19) and that you have an infinitely rich inheritance awaiting you (Ephesians 1). Remind yourself of these truths throughout the day and enjoy the freedom from things that this experience and ongoing awareness of God's love gives you.

Process this chapter. Together with your small group reflect on how this chapter impacted you. Did it convict, surprise, encourage, or discourage you? Reflect on your life in light of what you've learned. Do you feel you are following God's will in how you steward his resources? Are you reflecting his heart for the poor in how you spend your time and money? In what ways have you been influenced by the consumer culture of greed and the Powers that fuel it? If you and your Kingdom community were not disciples of Jesus, how would you spend your time and money differently than you now do?

Live out the generous Kingdom. Talk to God and those you're in community with about what steps you can take to more perfectly manifest the beauty of God's generous Kingdom and his heart for the poor. Here are a few suggestions for you and your community of fellow disciples to consider:

- Pray for the poor, especially those geographically closest to you. As you do this, repeatedly surrender all your possessions and money over to God. Let God reign over everything in your life, including your wallet and your possessions.

- Budget! A high percentage of Americans don't really know where their money goes. Remember that "your" money is really *God's* money—and you're his steward! Tally how much you spend on yourself versus how much you use to further the Kingdom and help the poor. Then enter into a dialogue with your Kingdom community and seek their help in discerning if the way you spend time and money is in accordance with God's will.

- If you live in a wealthy neighborhood, prayerful reflect on and discuss with others why you do so. Perhaps God has placed you there for Kingdom service, but perhaps you are living there simply because you like it and can afford it. That is normal for non-Kingdom people, but not for followers of Jesus. Seek God's will about where and how you're supposed to live.

- Wherever God has called you to live, seek his wisdom about how you can live more frugally and simply. It's okay to enjoy nonessential things God has blessed you with, but when we acquire or cling to things on the basis of our own preferences, they inhibit our capacity to manifest the beauty of the outrageously generous Kingdom. Seek the wisdom of your Kingdom community as you honestly ask yourself whether you're supposed to be "enjoying" that boat, cottage, or extra car. Are you supposed to have all those shoes and clothes? Many people testify that they've discovered a much greater depth of love, joy, and peace by dumping many of the "extras" and by living more simply.

- Whenever you consider purchasing an unnecessary item, ask

yourself, "Who might need this money more than I need this item?" If a person or a cause comes to mind, consider the possibility that God might be calling you to forgo the unnecessary item for the sake of that person or cause.

- If you are called to live in a wealthy neighborhood, consider ways you can alter your lifestyle so as to enter into meaningful relationships with the poor.

- If you're a westerner—and especially if you're an American—you live in a consumer culture that brainwashes people into believing they *need* to consume things to be happy and fulfilled. Learn about this consumer culture and seek out ways you can break free from it. A good place to start is watching a short video called *The Story of Stuff* at *storyofstuff.com*.

- Read up on poverty in your own country and around the world and process what you can learn with Kingdom people you share life with. (For suggested readings, see *www.gregboyd.org*.)

- Learn about various poverty and relief organizations. Find one or two to sacrificially give to, pray for, and perhaps volunteer in.

- As in the previous chapter, join with your small group and/or your church to host a party in which you invite "the poor, the crippled, the lame, the blind" (Luke 14:12–13). If you're part of a faith community that is relatively isolated from poverty, consider partnering with a faith community located in a poorer neighborhood.

- Go on short term mission trips to serve impoverished neighborhoods or in Third World countries. This is especially important for people who live in isolated wealthy communities since one can't be adequately impacted by poverty from lectures, books, or movies. One has to smell it, taste it, touch it, and breathe it.

- Volunteer regularly at a homeless shelter or soup kitchen.

- Go through your wardrobe and take out everything you haven't worn in the last twelve months and donate it to Goodwill, the Salvation Army, or another recycling clothing outlet that offers affordable or free clothes to the poor.

- If you can afford to do so, consider adopting an orphan from a Third World country.
- Whenever possible, purchase Fair Trade products. These are imported products for which a portion of the profit is reinvested in the economy of the impoverished community that helped produce the product.
- Unless specifically led by God to do so, I discourage people from giving to panhandlers. True, Jesus told us to give to everyone who asks (Luke 6:30), but this doesn't mean we have to give them precisely what they ask for. Statistically, it's likely you're helping support habits and activities that are helping to keep these people in poverty. Instead, I recommend taking strangers who approach you out to eat or to a grocery store. (One has to be wise about safety issues, of course.) Or consider carrying gift certificates to local eating establishments that you can offer people when they approach you for money.
- As discussed in chapter 6, as you pray blessings on people, be sensitive to the Spirit possibly leading you to engage in a random act of generosity.
- One of the best ways to help people in Third World countries is by extending them short-term loans to establish businesses. This is a relatively inexpensive way to make an enormous, life-long difference in the lives of impoverished individuals and their families. For more information, see *kiva.org/index.php*.
- If you participate in the political process, make poverty a primary issue in assessing the candidates and parties you support.

Help your church manifest the generous Kingdom. Talk to God and others about what your church can do to better revolt against the Powers that fuel greed and poverty, and what you can do to more thoroughly manifest the beauty of God's generous Kingdom. Here are some suggestions:

- Pray and think about whether your church looks like a "giant Jesus" in its relationship with the poor. What can you and others in your congregation do to help it become more like a collective Jesus in this area?

- Does your church's budget reflect God's heart for the poor? If it doesn't, use whatever influence you have to help make alleviating poverty a higher priority.
- Learn what your church is doing for the poor and become part of it. If it's doing little, talk to the leadership about starting a ministry to the poor.
- Volunteer to lead a book or film discussion group on poverty. A small group curriculum many churches have found helpful in waking Christians up to the biblical call to care for the poor is *Compassion By Command* (*www.compassionbycommand.com*).
- If you're in a suburban church, encourage the leadership of your church to enter into *mutually beneficial* partnerships with inner-city churches and volunteer to participate.
- Encourage the leadership to enter into relationships with other churches in your community to match resources and talents in the various churches with the needs in your community. A great ministry that helps churches around America do this is *Love in the Name of Christ* (Love INC). For information, go to *loveinc.org*. As with all other areas that are central to the Kingdom revolution, if the leadership of your church refuses to make confronting greed and poverty a high priority, prayerfully consider with your small group whether in fact this is the larger church body God is calling you to align with.

CHAPTER 12: THE REVOLT AGAINST THE ABUSE OF CREATION

Return to the Source. We mistreat the land and the animals entrusted to us primarily because we are self-oriented idolaters. To the extent that we are not full of the Life that comes from God alone, we tend to assign to nature only whatever value it has for *us*. Trees become little more than potential houses and paper while animals become little more than potential food and profits. We can only be freed to experience and appreciate the *intrinsic* value of nature and animals when we are freed from this idolatrous self-focus.

I encourage you, therefore, to continually return to the true source of Life. Spend time basking in God's love for you. Experience his reminders that you are perfectly justified by his grace (Romans 5:1), freed from all condemnation (Romans 8:1), blessed with every spiritual blessing (Ephesians 1:3), and are made to be his partner in caring for the earth. Together with your community of Jesus followers, engage in spiritual disciplines by which you help one another increasingly deepen your capacity to experience God's transforming Life and thus appreciate the intrinsic value of nature and the animal kingdom.

Process this chapter. Together with friends prayerfully reflect on this chapter. Did any of it convict, surprise, or confuse you? Do you feel you've been faithful to God's call to be a loving landlord of his earth and a faithful caregiver to his animals? How might you live differently because of what you've learned? Ask God to reveal ways in which your treatment of the earth's resources and of animals has been influenced by the norms of our consumer culture and by personal convenience rather than by God's revealed will.

Become a faithful landlord of God's creation. Talk to God and friends about the little ways you can be better stewards of God's resources. Remember, our primary Kingdom motivation is not utilitarian in nature (that is, the measurable difference we make in the world). Rather, our sole motivation is to be faithful to God's call. We are to have faith that every little thing we do to care for the environment makes a significant difference not because we can measure it but simply because we're advancing God's will "on earth as it is in heaven."

Here are a few practical suggestions for you and your Kingdom community to consider:

- One of the greatest sources of energy consumption and pollution is our use of cars. So I encourage you to drive less. Carpool with others. Ride the bus, bike, and, yes, walk whenever possible. Next time you purchase a car, buy one that uses less gas. If you can afford it, consider a hybrid, or, if you want to get really radical, do what my friend Shane Claiborne did: purchase (or make) a vehicle that runs on vegetable oil!

- Use less energy at home. Turn off lights when they're not in use. Use energy-saving light bulbs. Make your home more energy efficient. Lower your thermostat a degree or two in the winter and get used to wearing a sweater indoors. Run the air conditioner less in the summer and get used to sweating a little more indoors. The Kingdom is all about self-sacrifice.

- Conserve water. Water is a precious commodity, all the more so as the world's population grows and the globe warms. Don't run water when you're not using it. Take shorter showers and water your grass less often. (These resource-saving measures will also save you money. It might help keep you motivated to tally these savings and use them for some Kingdom cause.)

- If you choose to eat meat and use animal products (including eggs and dairy products), consider buying products produced on free-range farms rather than on factory farms (free-range farms are farms where animals are free to roam about and are treated humanely rather than being packed in overcrowded warehouses and abused). Free-range farms also tend to have much less negative impact on the environment than factory farms. For example, it takes a year's worth of shower water to produce a single pound of factory farm beef!

- Since growing, packaging, storing, and transporting food requires energy, buy seasonal, organically produced, locally grown food whenever possible.

- Consume less and waste less. For example, don't buy new clothes if used clothes will suffice. Upgrade your computer rather than buying a new one. Use both sides of paper. Never throw away good food. Buy refilled printer cartridges rather than new ones. Compost food scraps (or give them to your pet guinea pig like I do). Use your own coffee mug when out and about rather than going through paper or Styrofoam cups. Use bottled water as little as possible (its generally *not* healthier for you!) and recycle the bottles you do use.

- Join community environmental groups (litter pickup groups, gardening groups, etc.).
- Research and support a global organization dedicated to bringing clean water to people in need. Organizations like Lifewater International (*lifewater.org*), Africare (*africare.org*), Watercan (*watercan.com*), and Blood Water Mission (*bloodwatermission.com*) save lives by providing (among other things) wells and irrigation for needy villages.
- Buy environmentally friendly products (for tips, check out eco-friendly product websites such as *ecomall.com*).
- Become a student of environmental issues. Read up on and discuss these issues with others. (For suggested readings, see *gregboyd.org*.) Consider joining Christian environmental groups such as the Evangelical Environmental Network (*creationcare.org*) and Restoring Eden (*restoringeden.org*).
- If you choose to participate in the political process, be informed on environmental issues that are being debated and become knowledgeable about where various candidates stand on these issues.

Become a faithful animal caregiver. Consider committing to never participating in unnecessary violence toward animals by becoming a vegan or a vegetarian. (A vegan does not consume any animal products, including eggs, dairy products and honey, and does not use any animal-derived products such as fur, leather, and silk. A vegetarian commits to never eating any animal flesh but may eat eggs and dairy products and may use other animal products.)

Of course, this is not a biblical doctrine, for after the flood (Genesis 9:4) God allowed meat eating (drained of blood). Also, Jesus ate fish and possibly other meat (John 21:12–13). Nor does abstaining from meat make one more spiritual (I've met far too many subtly self-righteous vegans and vegetarians). On the other hand, refusing to participate in unnecessary violence toward animals manifests God's original nonviolent ideal for creation (Genesis 1:30) as well as the final nonviolent state of the world that will exist when the Kingdom has fully come (Isaiah 11:6–9). Moreover, while eating animals is a matter of survival in some situations, re-fraining from killing animals when we don't need to reflects greater mercy toward them.

Many people also find that veganism and vegetarianism have significant health benefits. My cholesterol level and weight both dropped significantly after I became a vegetarian, for example. Some find vegetarianism has spiritual benefits as well. I have found that my pledge of nonviolence toward animals has significantly in-creased my capacity to enjoy the intrinsic beauty of animals and nature and made me a more peaceful, peace-loving person.

Here are some practical suggestions on becoming a more faith-ful animal caregiver for you and your covenant community to consider:

- Purchase clothing, furniture, household items, and cosmetics produced without inflicting violence on animals. Information about animal-friendly products is available at such websites such as Leaping Bunny (*leapingbunny.org*) and Humanitaire (*shophumanitaire.com*).
- Some radical "animal rights" activists might want to tar and feather me for saying this, but if you can do so responsibly, consider owning pets. Aside from the personal and social benefits (see, for example, *petrealtynetwork.com*), caring for pets manifests the proper relationship humans were to have with the animal kingdom. When you love and care for an ani-mal, you manifest a little slice of the Kingdom! If you decide to acquire a pet, consider getting it from an animal shelter. If you choose to purchase one from a pet store, first investigate where the store acquires their animals from, since some pet store suppliers treat and breed animals in inhumane ways.
- Become a student of issues related to the treatment of ani-mals. Read and discuss these with others. Join a Christian group dedicated to the merciful treatment of animals. A good place to begin is *all-creatures.org* (though I should note that many of these groups are focused on political causes related to animal "rights").

CHAPTER 13: THE REVOLT AGAINST THE ABUSE OF SEX

Return to the Source. Paul says that the primary way we're transformed is by mentally gazing on the glory of God shining in the face of Jesus Christ (2 Corinthians 3:17–4:6). I don't believe we'll be able to swim upstream against the pervasive promiscuity of our culture in a healthy way unless we're being transformed by a compelling vision of Christ's love and are continually finding all of our worth, significance, and security in him.

Make regular dates to be with Jesus and allow the Holy Spirit to point you to the beautiful, living Lord (John 15:26; 16:13–14). Cultivate a Life-giving relationship with him throughout the day. Talk to him and listen for him to talk to you. Continually remind yourself that you're surrounded by his love at every moment. Regularly engage in worship experiences and the spiritual disciplines with a community of like-minded Jesus followers. Your revolt against the diabolic Powers that fuel immorality will only be as successful as your relationship with Christ is vibrant.

Process this chapter. Reflect with friends on the material in this chapter and how it has impacted you. Did any of it convict, surprise, encourage, or discourage you? Prayerfully reflect on your past sexual behavior in light of what you've learned. How will you live your life differently?

Repent and restore. If you've been involved in sexual sin, I encourage you to confess it to God and repent of it. Repentance (*metanoia*) doesn't mean you necessarily feel remorse for past sins. This is a common and unfortunate misunderstanding, leading some to think that unless one *feels* deep regret their repentance isn't genuine. The fact is that what we feel is largely the result of our cultural conditioning. Consequently, in our promiscuous culture people often don't feel that sex before or outside of marriage is wrong— even when they *believe* it is.

Some pastors (especially youth pastors) try to motivate Christians to stay pure by telling them that if they engage in sexual sin they're going to feel miserable. This argument sometimes backfires, however, for Western Christians often feel great about their sexual encounters. I've even had people tell me that a particular sexual relationship outside of marriage "feels blessed by God." When these people discover their pastor is wrong about what they'd feel, they sometimes conclude that the pastor is mistaken in telling them sex outside of marriage is wrong.

The truth is, feelings are not reliable indicators of truth. Our motivation for obeying God shouldn't be based on what we feel.

Repentance simply means "to turn." It may be motivated by feelings of regret, but it may be motivated by the fact that a person now understands that a certain behavior is wrong. When we understand the importance of honoring the sign of the marriage covenant and that our past sexual activity has been sinful, it's time for us to turn from it—regardless of how we *feel*.

Repentance may also involve making amends. When Zacchaeus, the tax collector, repented of his thievery, he committed himself to paying people back more than he had stolen from them (Luke 19:8). Restoring things isn't about paying for our past sins, for our sins are forgiven the moment we confess them and repent. Rather, it's about bringing closure to things we've done by making them right, insofar as this is possible.

When we have sex with people outside of wedlock, we not only dishonor God and desecrate the sign of the covenant, we also violate the people we had sex with. It's often appropriate, therefore, to ask forgiveness not only from God but also from the people we have wronged. Many find this humble act to be profoundly healing and liberating.

Of course, bringing up the past with those we've wronged isn't always possible or wise, especially if the past sexual partner is now married. It's thus important to seek guidance from God and others before doing this.

Receive forgiveness. Once we've asked for forgiveness from God, it's important to trust that he has given it. Scripture promises us that "if we confess our sins, [God] is faithful and just and will forgive us our sins and purify us from all unrighteousness" (1 John

1:9). On faith, we need to accept that our sin has been completely forgiven and our unrighteousness removed.

Here too, we should not treat our feelings as if they were reliable indicators of truth. For a variety of reasons, certain people may have lingering feelings of guilt even after they've confessed their sin. If they're not careful, the accuser (Revelation 12:10) can use this to drive them into self-condemnation. Some are driven back into immoral sexual activity because of this, especially if their sexual activity was used to medicate pain in their life (as it often is).

If you continue to feel guilty after repenting, I encourage you to confess your sin to fellow disciples with whom you are in relationship. Allow them to speak God's forgiveness to you. As Dietrich Bonhoeffer observed, we sometimes experience Christ most powerfully through the words and actions of fellow disciples.[4] I also encourage you to be transformed by the daily renewal of your mind (Romans 12:2). Throughout the day, recite passages such as 1 John 1:9, reminding yourself that you are completely forgiven.[5]

Be immersed in community. Behind Western culture's fall into sexual decadence is the mantra "My sex life is nobody's business but mine." The advent of the birth-control pill, which itself was part of the sexual revolution of the '60s, helped divorce sex from social consequences. This fed the intense individualism and moral relativism of our culture, creating our present privatized, recreational view of sex.

People may talk about their sex life all they want—often shamelessly flaunting their sexual exploits on blogs or in books—but so long as "no one gets hurt," the current thinking goes, no one can question anyone else's sexual activity. This is a distinctly modern perspective. Traditionally, it has been understood by all cultures that the welfare of the general public hangs on the preservation of sexual morals. Everyone's sexual fidelity *is*, to this degree, everyone's business. In the West we have lost this communal wisdom.[6]

Whether married or single, all who take the Bible's call to live a chaste life seriously need people in their lives whom they trust enough to give permission to ask tough questions about their sexual behavior. Especially in a culture such as ours in which we're bombarded with relentless lies about sex and in which temptations lie in wait at every turn, we need people to notice when something in our life is going astray and who care enough to confront us.

Here's a broader application of this principle I'd encourage single people to adopt: don't do anything sexually with another person in private that you wouldn't do in public.

The privacy of sexual intimacy is a unique privilege of the "one flesh" marriage covenant. It's part of the precious diamond married couples share. A married couple gets to enjoy each other in ways that would be totally inappropriate in public. The married couple has purchased this privilege, as it were, by pledging their lives to one another. Outside of this covenant, I would argue, no one has a right to privacy regarding their sex life, at least not from a Kingdom perspective. Make the general public your accountability partner.

I'm aware that this probably sounds Victorian, repressive, mean, and unfair to people conditioned by the Western "sex-is-recreation" mindset. But for Kingdom revolutionaries, that should be considered one more piece of evidence that it's saying something right!

CHAPTER 14: THE REVOLT AGAINST SECULARISM

Return to the Source. Your revolt against secularism is only possible to the degree that your innermost being is nourished by the Life found in Christ alone. As long as we crave idols, our attention will remain imprisoned. Commit yourself to getting your worth, significance, and security from Christ. Throughout the day remind yourself of your identity in him and express prayers of gratitude for who God made you to be.

Introspection. Alone and with friends, honestly reflect on the extent to which your confession of Christ as Lord has been merely theoretical. To what degree do you live, think, and experience the world moment-by-moment as a functional atheist? If you discern that you have, in fact, been entrapped in the secular worldview, don't judge yourself. That is never helpful. Simply return to practicing the presence of God in this moment. What matters is not how many past moments have or have not been surrendered to God. The only thing that matters is that *this* moment is surrendered to God—and now *this* moment.

Practice the presence. While we need to cultivate an awareness of God's presence on a moment-by-moment basis, it's helpful to set aside special times to engage in this spiritual discipline. Carve out a segment of time in which you stop all other activity and simply become aware that you are surrounded by God's eternal, perfect, unconditional love. Attend to the details of what you see, hear, touch, smell, and perhaps taste in this moment, but do so against the backdrop of this infinite love. In other words, allow God's loving presence to be the canvas on which your experience of the world is painted. See how long you can remain aware of his presence. When you notice that God's presence has drifted out of your awareness, don't get frustrated with yourself. Just become aware, once again, that you are engulfed in his perfect love.

Along the same lines, many people have found it helpful—and sometimes revolutionary—to go on a silent retreat. These can last anywhere from a day to a week. The goal of these retreats is to take a break from the business of our ordinary lives, to quiet one's mind, and to grow in one's capacity to remain continually aware of God's loving presence.

Reminders of God's Presence. Our secularized lives run on habit. Almost all of our thoughts, whether we're conscious of it or not, are determined by habit. This is why remaining aware of God's presence on a moment-by-moment basis is so challenging. To counter this, consider putting Post-it notes in places you come upon during the day: the bathroom mirror, inside your front door, the car steering wheel, the refrigerator, and other places. Let them remind you to wake up to God's presence that surrounds you in that moment.

Act on a nudge. As you train yourself to listen to God throughout the day, commit to spontaneously responding to inner promptings you receive. I encourage you to begin by doing at least one thing each day that you hadn't planned on doing. You'll find that spontaneously acting on these impulses sometimes brings about what I call "Kingdom coincidences," that is, you do or say something that just lands perfectly in the moment, and it's evident that the prompting is not "just you." Over time you begin to develop an ability to discern what is and is not "just you" (though we always need to remain humble and careful not to assume our thoughts and impulses are from God).

NOTES

CHAPTER 1: GIANT JESUS

[1] See, for example, John 13:15; Ephesians 5:1–2; 1 Peter 2:20–21; 1 John 2:6. Many today embrace the erroneous view that getting "saved" is about avoiding hell. The biblical concept of salvation is not about avoiding the *consequences* of sin (hell) but about being freed from the *sin* that leads to those consequences. It's about being empowered to walk in a Kingdom way that leads to eternal life, not death. This is why the New Testament speaks of salvation as something that *has* happened, *is* happening, and *will* happen. When I speak of salvation, or "being saved," throughout this book, *this* is what I mean.

[2] This sermon series can be found at *whchurch.org/content/page_721.htm*. The story was later picked up by the *New York Times* (July 30, 2006) and can be found at *nytimes.com/2006/07/30/us/30pastor.html*. This sermon series formed the foundation for my book *The Myth of a Christian Nation: How the Quest for Political Power is Destroying the Church* (Grand Rapids, Mich.: Zondervan, 2006).

[3] The term "Christian" was used by non-Christians in the New Testament to refer to followers of Jesus (Acts 26:28; cf. 11:26). Never did Jesus-followers refer to themselves as "Christian." Given the significant negative associations many today have with the label, I prefer to refer to followers of Jesus simply as "Jesus followers" or "Kingdom people," though I'll occasionally use the word "Christian" in contexts where its true meaning is understood.

[4] Following the pattern of the New Testament, I'm using the word *church* (Greek, *ecclesia*) to refer to the tribe of those who have responded to God's call to live differently from the world by pledging their lives to Jesus. I'm not using the word to refer to any identifiable human institution.

CHAPTER 2: CHRIST AND CAESAR

[1] Early Christians often pointed to the uniform commitment of Christians to love their enemies rather than use violence against them as proof that Jesus is Lord. It was, I believe, a profoundly biblical apologetic. See, for example, Justin Martyr, "Dialogue with Trypho," *Ante-Nicene Fathers*, Alexander Rob-

erts and James Donaldson, eds. (Peabody, Mass: Hendrickson, 1999 [1885]), Vol. 1, 254; Tertullian, "An Answer to Jews," *Ante-Nicene Fathers*, Vol. I, 154; Origen, "Against Celsus," *Ante-Nicene Fathers*, Vol. 4, 558. For a classic overview of Christians' attitudes toward the use of violence throughout history, highlighting the uniform pacifism of the early church, see Ronald H. Bainton, *Christian Attitudes toward War and Peace: A Historical Survey and Critical Reevaluation* (Nashville: Abingdon, 1960).

[2] On the meaning of Jesus' ironic command to "give to Caesar what belongs to Caesar," see *Myth of a Christian Nation*, and Shane Claiborne and Chris Haw, *Jesus For President* (Grand Rapids: Zondervan, 2008).

[3] On the other hand, some make a rather compelling case for Christians to abstain from voting as a matter of principle. See Ted Lewis, ed., *Electing Not to Vote: Christian Reflections on Reasons for Not Voting* (Eugene, Ore.: Wipf and Stock, 2008). In America where so many mistakenly assume it's a "Christian's duty" to vote, this perspective desperately needs to be heard.

[4] See Gregory Boyd, *God at War: The Bible and Spiritual Conflict* (Downers Grove, Ill.: InterVarsity, 1997), especially chapters 2 and 3.

[5] On the apocalyptic worldview, see N. T. Wright, *The New Testament and the People of God* (Minneapolis: Fortress, 1992), especially 280–99, and Boyd, *God at War*, 172–80

[6] For a discussion on illness and deformities as demonically caused, see Boyd, *God at War*, 182–84.

[7] Here I'm following the example of Walter Wink in his acclaimed trilogy, The Powers. See especially Walter Wink, *Naming the Powers: The Language of Power in the New Testament* (Philadelphia: Fortress, 1984).

CHAPTER 4: THE REVOLT AGAINST JUDGMENT

[1] For a full development and defense of the relationship between judgment and "the Tree of the Knowledge of Good and Evil," see Gregory A. Boyd, *Repenting of Religion: Turning from Judgment to the Love of God* (Grand Rapids: Baker, 2004).

CHAPTER 5: THE REVOLT AGAINST RELIGION

[1] For those who might be interested, I wrote about the beliefs and practices of this brand of Christianity in a book entitled *Oneness Pentecostals and the Trinity* (Grand Rapids: Baker, 1992).

[2] On a few of the more notorious moments in church history where "Christians" were involved in perpetrating violence and slaughter, see Joseph Perez and Janet Lloyd, *The Spanish Inquisition: A History* (New Haven: Yale University Press, 2006); Christopher Tyerman, *God's War: A New History*

of the Crusades (Cambridge, Mass.: Belknap, 2006); David Nirenberg, *Communities of Violence* (Princeton: Princeton University Press, 1998). For a succinct overview, see "Chamber of Horrors" in Bruxy Cavey, *The End of Religion: Encountering the Subversive Spirituality of Jesus* (Colorado Springs: NavPress, 2007), chap. 4.

3 For a good account of this, see Ronald H. Bainton, *Hunted Heretic: The Life and Death of Servetus* (Boston: Beacon, 1953).

4 On the persecution and martyrdom of Anabaptists see Thieleman Van Braqt and Joseph F. Sohm, *Martyrs Mirror*, 2nd reprint ed. (Scotdale, Penn.: Herald, 2001).

5 See David Kinnaman and Gabe Lyons, *unChristian: What a New Generation Thinks about Faith … and Why It Matters* (Grand Rapids: Baker, 2007), for an overview of non-Christian perception of Evangelicals.

CHAPTER 6: THE REVOLT AGAINST INDIVIDUALISM

1 Our main ministry is called Providence Ministries, and it was started by Marcia and Greg Erickson (*providenceinhaiti.blogspot.com*).

2 R. C. Kessler, "Prevalence, Severity, and Unmet Need for Treatment of Mental Disorders in the World Health Organization World Mental Health Surveys," *Journal of the American Medical Association*, 291/21 (2004): 2581–90; J. Colla, S. Buka, D. Harrington, and J. M. Murphy, "Depression and Modernization: A Cross-cultural Study of Women," *Social Psychiatry and Psychiatric Epidemiology* 41/4 (2006): 271–79.

CHAPTER 7: THE REVOLT AGAINST NATIONALISM

1 For information on this ministry, go to *goodnewstour.com*.

CHAPTER 8: THE REVOLT AGAINST VIOLENCE

1 This event is depicted in the award-winning French film *Joyeux Noel* and thoroughly discussed in Stanley Weintraub, *Silent Night: The Story of the World War I Christmas Truce* (New York: Plume, 2002).

2 *Raca* was an expression used to call someone "worthless."

3 Something similar could be said of Jesus' command to offer one's coat to anyone who demands your coat and going the extra mile when someone forces you to go one. See Walter Wink, *Engaging the Powers* (Minneapolis: Augsburg, 1992), 175–84.

4 Space doesn't permit delving into the thorny issue of how to reconcile the Old and New Testaments on the issue of how to respond to enemies. For several perspectives, see C. S. Cowles, E. M. Merrill, D. L. Gard, T. Longman

III, in *Show Them NO Mercy: Four Views on God and Canaanite Genocide* (Grand Rapids: Zondervan, 2003); P. Craigie, *The Problem of War in the Old Testament* (Eugene: Wipf and Stock, 2002 [1978]); V. Eller, *War and Peace: From Genesis to Revelation* (Eugene: Wipf and Stock, 2003 [1981]). Right now I would simply emphasize that Christians are called to base their view of God and their lifestyle on Jesus, not the Old Testament.

CHAPTER 10: THE REVOLT AGAINST RACISM

[1] I continue to speak of "race" and "racial reconciliation" only because this is how most people continue to speak, and it's therefore the most effective way of identifying the issues that need to be confronted.

[2] For example, Luke 9:52–54; 10:30–37; 17:11–19; John 4.

[3] I apologize to my non-American readers for my restricted focus at this point. But racial dynamics differ significantly from country to country and are highly complex. I can only speak with confidence about the specifics of the race dynamics in my own country.

CHAPTER 11: THE REVOLT AGAINST POVERTY AND GREED

[1] Ronald J. Sider, *Rich Christians in an Age of Hunger: Moving from Affluence to Generosity* (Nashville: Nelson, 2005), 24–25.

CHAPTER 12: THE REVOLT AGAINST THE ABUSE OF CREATION

[1] I know it's heresy to many to even raise this possibility, but there are actually some interesting (though mostly ignored) arguments calling this into question. See, for example, Bjorn Lomborg, *Cool It: The Skeptical Environmentalist's Guide to Global Warming* (New York: Knopf, 2007); Patrick J. Michaels, ed. *Shattered Consensus: The True State of Global Warming* (New York: Rowman and Littlefield, 2005); S. Fred Singer and Dennis T. Avery, *Unstoppable Global Warming—Every 1,500 Years* (New York: Rowman and Littlefield, 2007). For my part, I'm not convinced either way.

[2] There's a number of ways to reconcile this biblical teaching with the scientific evidence of millions of years of violence in creation leading up to the creation of humans. See, for example, Gregory A. Boyd, *Satan and the Problem of Evil: Developing a Trinitarian Warfare Theodicy* (Downers Grove, Ill.: InterVarsity, 2001) 293–318; and "Evolution as Cosmic Warfare: A Biblical Perspective on 'Natural' Evil," in Thomas J. Oord, ed., *Creation Made Free: Open Theology Engaging Science* (Eugene, Ore.: Wipf and Stock, 2009).

[3] I go into much greater depth on this in an essay entitled "Satan and the Corruption of Nature: Seven Arguments" at *gregboyd.org/essays/apologetics /problem-of-evil/satan-and-the-corruption-of-nature-seven-arguments/*, and *Satan and the Problem of Evil*, 242–318.

[4] See Boyd, *God at War*, 182–84; E. Yamauchi, "Magic or Miracle? Diseases, Demons and Exorcisms," in *The Miracles of Jesus*, eds. D. Wenham and C. Blomberg, (Sheffield: JSOT Press, 1986), 90–93; P. Davids, "Sickness and Suffering in the New Testament," in *Wrestling with Dark Angels*, ed. C. P. Wagner and F. Pennoyer (Ventura: Regal, 1990), 215–17; and J. Kallas, *The Significance of the Synoptic Miracles* (Greenwich, Conn: Seabury, 1961).

[5] Alfred Lord Tennyson, "In Memoriam," LVI, in Christopher Ricks, ed., *The New Oxford Book of Victorian Verse* (Oxford: Oxford University Press, 1987), 27.

[6] See, for example, Richard Dawkins, *The Devil's Chaplain: Reflections on Hope, Lies, Science and Love* (New York: Mariner, 2005). For a more in depth discussion of natural evil and various responses to it, see Boyd, *Satan and the Problem of Evil*, chapters 8–10.

[7] Howard Bloom, *The Lucifer Principle: A Scientific Expedition into the Forces of History* (New York: Atlantic Monthly Press, 1995), 2.

[8] See Boyd, *Satan and the Problem of Evil*, 39–49, 294–95.

[9] This doesn't mean he wasn't *also* symbolizing the impending judgment of Israel, as commentators uniformly hold.

[10] For a fuller discussion, see Boyd, *God at War*, 205–13.

[11] For an introduction, I strongly encourage readers to view the film *From Farm to Fridge* (*chooseveg.com/animal-cruelty.asp*). Other informative exposés on factory farms are *We Are Awake* (http://weareawake.ning.com/video); *Factory Farming Campaign* (http://www.hsus.org/farm/multimedia/); and *Pig Farm Cruelty Revealed* (http://www.peta.org/feat/invest/index.html). For book recommendations, see *gregboyd.org*.

CHAPTER 13: THE REVOLT AGAINST THE ABUSE OF SEX

[1] There is much debate over Jesus' exception clause in Matthew 19:9 ("... anyone who divorces his wife, except for sexual immorality"). I'm most persuaded by those arguments that suggest that the exception clause refers to the betrothal period in which a man and woman were *legally* married but had not yet become "one flesh." See J. Wenham and W. E. Heth, *Jesus and Divorce* (Nashville: Nelson, 1985) 169–78. There's also much debate over what Jesus means when he says a divorced man who marries another woman "commits adultery" (Matthew 19:9). In my view, Jesus was again confronting self-righteousness attitudes by reminding his audience of God's ideal for

people to have a single, lifelong "one flesh" relationship. Even *thinking about* sexual activity outside of this ideal technically constitutes "adultery" (Matthew 5:28). But Jesus wasn't thereby revoking the Old Testament's permission to get remarried. Indeed, Jesus seems to *assume* that a divorced woman will get remarried, despite the fact that it falls short of God's ideal (Matthew 5:32).

[2] See Deuteronomy 22:13–17, for example.

CHAPTER 14: THE REVOLT AGAINST SECULARISM

[1] Though, interestingly enough, there is evidence the Western worldview is beginning to change. The last several decades have witnessed an explosion of interest in Eastern and pagan religions as well as the occult. This is generally referred to as "the New Age Movement."

[2] Brother Lawrence, *The Practice of the Presence of God* (New Kensington, Penn.: Whitaker, 1982).

[3] If you'd like to explore the practice of the presence of God in more depth, see my forthcoming book, *This Sacred Moment: Reflections on Practicing the Presence of God* (Grand Rapids: Zondervan, 2009).

WHAT CAN WE DO? AN ACTION GUIDE

[1] On the practice of resting in Christ, see G. Boyd, *Seeing Is Believing: The Transforming Power of Imaginative Prayer* (Grand Rapids: Baker, 2004).

[2] By the way, you will find you are much better at discussing theological "hot topics" with others in a calm, loving manner when you are freed of religious idolatry. Religious (as well as political) debates become acrimonious primarily because some element of the person's core worth or security is being leveraged on the outcome.

[3] Wink, *Engaging the Powers*, 317.

[4] Dietrich Bonhoeffer, *Life Together: A Discussion of Christian Fellowship* (New York: HarperCollins, 1954), 110–22.

[5] For example, Romans 4:7; Colossians 2:13–15; Hebrews 10:18.

[6] For a profound analysis on how autonomous individualism came to define American culture as well as on how it is now destroying American culture, see Wendell Berry, *Sex, Economy, Community and Freedom: Eight Essays* (New York: Pantheon, 1992).

Share Your Thoughts

With the Author: Your comments will be forwarded to the author when you send them to *zauthor@zondervan.com*.

With Zondervan: Submit your review of this book by writing to *zreview@zondervan.com*.

Free Online Resources at
www.zondervan.com

Zondervan AuthorTracker: Be notified whenever your favorite authors publish new books, go on tour, or post an update about what's happening in their lives.

Daily Bible Verses and Devotions: Enrich your life with daily Bible verses or devotions that help you start every morning focused on God.

Free Email Publications: Sign up for newsletters on fiction, Christian living, church ministry, parenting, and more.

Zondervan Bible Search: Find and compare Bible passages in a variety of translations at www.zondervanbiblesearch.com.

Other Benefits: Register yourself to receive online benefits like coupons and special offers, or to participate in research.